The Langworthys
OF
DUBUQUE

THE KEY CITY'S FIRST FAMILY

SUSAN MILLER HELLERT

THE
History
PRESS

Published by The History Press
Charleston, SC
www.historypress.com

First published 2021

Manufactured in the United States

ISBN 9781467148504

Library of Congress Control Number: 2021945855

This book is dedicated to my family for their support, assistance and tolerance.

IN THE BEGINNING

*T*he Langworthys can rightly be called the "First Family of Dubuque." Their history and the early history of Dubuque—in fact, the early history of the United States—have been closely aligned. When important events occurred in U.S. history, one or more members of the Langworthy family was there. They exemplified the frontier spirit. Wandering west always in search of a better life filled their life stories with adventure. They faced hardships, disease, hard work, accident, war and death during that search. They also found love, home, family, friendship and wealth.

By the time the family arrived at the Dubuque Lead Mines in the late 1820s, the ancestors of the family had participated in much of this nation's early history as well as England's. King Henry VIII had granted the Langworthy family their coat of arms, depicting a stag with three greyhounds, in the sixteenth century. The name Langworthy began as Langworthe: an old English word meaning a long or large village. Langworthe was a parish in Devon, England, in what is today Dartmoor National Park. The name Langworthe was first recorded in 1468, when surnames became necessary because governments began to impose personal taxes.

Andrew Langworthy, born in Widecombe in the Moor, Devon, England, on November 30, 1610, to Richard and Gwen Langworthy, arrived in Newport, Rhode Island, in 1652. Rhode Island had been founded only sixteen years earlier in 1636 at Providence by Roger Williams, Anne Hutchinson and others who had been expelled from the Massachusetts

Colony because they adhered to a belief in religious toleration and the separation of church and state. Andrew's baptism occurred at the "mill" in 1652. He was declared a "freeman" in 1856. He then married Rachel Hubbard in 1658. This began the American Langworthy family saga. Rachel, born in 1642, in Springfield, Massachusetts, was the daughter of Samuel and Tacy Cooper Hubbard. Samuel, a zealous Baptist, traveled to Boston in 1657 to "vest bretherin who was imprisoned in the Boston jayl for witnessing the truths of baptizing believers only: Brothers John Clarke, Obadiah Homes, and John Crandall." In 1664, he became the general solicitor of the colony. Samuel and Tacy withdrew from the First Baptist Church founded by Roger Williams and his followers in 1638 in Newport. They along with several followers and their children formed the Seventh Day Baptist Church in December 1671.

Andrew and Rachel had ten children. Very little is known about most of them. In 1688, seven of the children were listed as living, with three deceased. Their eldest child is known only as "M" from a broken gravestone in the Hubbard family cemetery. He died at the age of sixteen. Samuel (1659–1716), now regarded as the eldest, lived in Newport and Kings Town and owned large tracts of land in the Narragansett region of Rhode Island. Samuel married Rachel in 1680. His sailing career took him often to the West Indies. Both Samuel and Rachel died in 1716. Andrew (1675–1720) married Patience Brownell in 1709. John (1661–1700) married Elizabeth Witter, and James (1680–1720) married Mary Remington. Mary's father was Captain Stephen Remington of the Jamestown, Newport County Rhode Island Militia. The militia fought in King Philip's War. It is interesting to note that when James died in 1720, his estate included feather and silk bed blankets, coverlets and pillows; one large frying pan; four augers; two candlesticks; one tramel (an instrument or device, sometimes of leather, more usually of rope, fitted to a horse's legs to restrict his motions and force him to walk slowly); one iron pot; two old chests; one gun; and two swords. Listed first, the bed blankets and coverlets were undoubtedly considered the most valuable, since no industrial process for making cloth existed yet. All cloth had to be homemade or imported and, therefore, was of great value.

King Philip's War, named for Metacom, the chief of the Wampanoag who took the English name of Philip, is considered the costliest of America's wars. In 1675, the indigenous peoples of New England embarked on their last-ditch attempt to oust the English colonists from their lands. Due to encroachment on their land by the colonists, the demand by the colonists that the Indians surrender their guns and the trial and execution of two Wampanoag for the murder of another Wampanoag despite this being a violation of Wampanoag law, the Indians began a series of raids across New England. When the war ended, thousands of indigenous people were dead or wounded, had been sold into slavery/indentured servitude or had fled to the Iroquois to the north or the Abenakis to the west. About 1,200 colonists' homes had been burned, crops were destroyed and one-tenth of the adult male colonial population had been killed. It is estimated that 60 to 80 percent of the total Indian population in New England had been eliminated. The economy of New England had been destroyed; its recovery took fifty years. The American colonists fought the war and suffered the losses on their own with no help from England. This fact caused the colonists to question the value of being part of the British empire.

Solon Langworthy (1814–1886) in later years wrote about the mystery concerning one of the Langworthy ancestors known as Theophilius Whale (or Josiah Whaley or Edward Whalley). During the English civil war of the 1600s that resulted in the beheading of King Charles I, Theophilius, who was a judge, participated by signing the death certificate for Charles I. In 1660, when the Commonwealth established by Oliver Cromwell collapsed and the monarchy was restored by Charles II, Theophilius had a price on his head. As a result, he secretly fled England for Virginia. There he met and married Elizabeth Mills. They moved to Rhode Island in 1679 permanently. They lived a secluded and secret life there and even refused to educate their children despite Theophilius's own excellent education—he knew Hebrew, Greek and Latin. He always believed that his "misfortunes" resulted from his extensive education. Theophilius died at Hopkins Hill, Rhode Island, in 1720 at the age of 103. The mystery deepens as both he and his wife were buried in the same unmarked grave. Sometime between 1900 and 1990, a gravestone appeared on their grave. No one knows to this day who erected it or why. The memorial reads, "Here was buried Theophilius, The singular good man; Born in England 1616; Died on this hill 1720; and his wife Elizabeth Mills of Virginia. Their descendents endure even unto this day." Historians have never been able to prove if Theophilius was actually Josiah Whaley or Edward Whalley or Theophilius Whale—or perhaps he was none of these and was really Robert Whaley, Theophilius's brother. Robert served as a guard for King Charles I, but during the English civil war, he participated in the actual execution of Charles I, so he either was executed after 1660 or escaped to the colonies. No one knows. Solon definitely believed the family stories that they were related.

James Langworthy II (1711–1762), grandson of Andrew and son of James and Mary, supported the American Whig movement, which opposed absolute monarchy. For these beliefs, British Regulars during the French and Indian War of 1754–63 destroyed and plundered the home of James and Sarah Langworthy. His grandson, Dr. Augustus Langworthy, explained of James:

> *They lived in a cottage or farmhouse built after the model of the old English with a long capacious kitchen with bedrooms attached on the same floor and a front hall. It was a rule with him to have placed every night four large buckets full of water in the entry. One night when the family was all rapt in sleep he was awakened by a suffocating smoke coming through cracks in the door that opened into the kitchen. He ascertained that the interior of the kitchen was in flames and filled with dense smoke. He aroused his family, threw the beds out of a window and the children upon them then made his way through the long kitchen to the front entry. With the four buckets of water there placed he extinguished the flames and saved the house.*

Their son, James Langworthy III (1752–1800), served as an indentured servant to first Benjamin Green in 1766 and then Thomas Green in 1769 in Rhode Island. When freed of indenture, he was given a set of "Freedom Clothes" and began a career in seafaring and fishing. His employment took him to the Gulf of St. Lawrence, Philadelphia and the West Indies (Caribbean Islands). His son, Dr. Augustus Langworthy, wrote that "by his [James] studious habits he acquired by firelight a good knowledge of navigation and nautical science, though he previously had no scholastic education except what he acquired by firelight during hours devoted to sleep; but, he became a good scholar in mathematics and had an extensive knowledge of geography, astronomy, history etc. He was always a republican in feeling." His seafaring career came to an end with the American Revolutionary War.

James served in the Revolutionary War as a private in Captain Samuel S. Sawyer's Company, Colonel Ebenezer Wood's Vermont Regiment. On one expedition to Crown Point and Ticonderoga, James barely escaped death from starvation and cold. His uncle on his mother's side of the family, Simester (first name unknown), froze to death crossing the Green Mountains on this same trip. Ethan Allen, Seth Warner and the Green Mountain Boys of Vermont, along with Captain Benedict Arnold of the

Connecticut militia, captured Fort Ticonderoga and its seventy British soldiers on May 10, 1775. Fort Crown Point, guarded by only nine British soldiers, fell two days later. In 1776, both sites returned to British control under General John Burgoyne. Despite Burgoyne's defeat in October 1777 at the Battle of Saratoga in New York, both forts remained in British hands until the end of the American Revolution.

James married Anna Deen of Connecticut on April 5, 1775, and moved to Windsor, Vermont. James Langworthy died of typhoid fever within an hour of his seven-year-old son Jonathon's death of the same disease in 1800. Typhoid was the scourge of the frontier. Also known as bilious fever, typhoid is spread by bacteria in food or water contaminated by an infected person's feces or urine. In a society where water was usually secured from shallow wells or open sources and with haphazard sanitation, typhoid claimed many lives. James's widow was left to cope with their thirteen remaining children. Anna Deen Langworthy died in 1839 at the age of eighty-seven in the home of her daughter Anna Simmonds in Potsdam, New York. Dr. Augustus Langworthy wrote of his father, James, "Often, very often, I have heard him mourn the blot of slavery on our national escutcheon [shield] and indulge in fearful forebodings of its pernicious influence in the future upon the policy and politics of the nation." He had issued a prophetic pronouncement for the young nation, sadly.

One of James and Anna's sons, Phineas, who was born in 1782, traveled the world as a lecturer and teacher. He spent a great deal of time teaching in the East Indies (Indonesia).

Another son, Jonathan, born in 1783, served with the American forces during the Revolutionary War. He sailed on the brigantine *Angelica*, which carried sixteen guns. In May 1778, the British ship *Andromeda*, with twenty-eight guns, captured the *Angelica*. Those captured, including Jonathan Langworthy, were committed to Forton Prison near Portsmouth, New Hampshire, on July 7, 1778. The prison had been a hospital until it was replaced by one of newer and improved construction. One prisoner at Forton explained, "We had nothing to eat but boiled cabbage." The prisoners also lacked adequate clothing, as their possessions were seized upon capture. According to the same prisoner, many men were "half naked." Finally, in November 1777, the British Admiralty responded to complaints of insufficient food and clothing, but quantity and quality still remained deficient.

Stephen Langworthy, son of James and Anna, was born in Windsor, Vermont, on October 4, 1777. A graduate of Yale Medical School, Stephen married Betsey Woodbury Massey on November 10, 1798. Betsey gave birth to twelve children from 1800 to 1817: James Lyon, Stephen, Ella Eliza, Laura, Lucius Hart, Edward, May Ann, Sarah Maria, Lucretia C., Solon Massey, Lucien and Harriet Lyon.

Stephen enlisted in the army during the War of 1812. He worked as an army physician and surgeon during the Battles of Plattsburgh and Sacket's Harbor. The American victory at the Battle of Sacket's Harbor (May 29, 1813) on Lake Ontario repulsed the British attempt to seize the principal dockyard for the American naval squadron on the Great Lakes. The Battle of Plattsburgh, from September 6 to September 11, 1814, ended the final invasion of the northern states by Britain. British forces planned to converge on Plattsburgh, New York, but were defeated by American forces led by Brigadier General Macomb and Master Commandant Macdonough. Due to the victory at Plattsburgh, the British lost any leverage they might have had during the peace negotiations at Ghent to maintain territory in the United States since none had been retained at the end of hostilities. (This rule is known as *Uti possidetis*.)

Stephen and Betsey Langworthy joined the throngs of pioneers who continually moved west. In their case, these moves went from Vermont to Hopkinton, New York, due to the unsettled conditions on the Canadian border and the difficulty supporting a large family in a relatively unsettled area. They then moved to Western Pennsylvania at French Creek and on to Illinois. The move to Missouri and finally Iowa completed their frontier journey.

Reodolophus Langworthy (1787–1820), Stephen's brother, left home with his brothers Augustus and Cyrus in 1812 to seek his fortune. Upon his return, he married in 1817 and settled in Alton, Illinois, where he served as a justice of the peace. Sadly, he drowned in the Mississippi River at the age of thirty-three.

Augustus (1788–1866) returned to settle in Upper Alton, Illinois, in 1817. He had worked in the brickyards in Cincinnati and traveled to New Orleans. He even studied medicine in Virginia. He married Adah Meacham in 1818. He practiced medicine at Fort Crawford, Illinois (Peoria), in 1824. While with the Peoria Volunteers during the Black Hawk War, Augustus functioned as the army surgeon. He then moved to Bureau Junction, Illinois, where he bought a large tract of land. After his wife died in 1836, he decided to give up the practice of medicine to concentrate on farming. It had become difficult to practice medicine in such a remote and sparsely settled region. He married Adelia Perkins in 1837. One of their sons, Lewis Cass, died at the Battle of Vicksburg on July 3, 1863. Buried in a trench on the battlefield, his body was never recovered. An officer's commission had been sent for him, but unluckily, he died before it arrived.

Augustus James Langworthy Jr. (1826–1910), the eldest son of Augustus and Adah, traveled to Oregon via the Oregon Trail in a wagon pulled by horses and oxen. He left Peoria on April 7, 1847, and arrived at Oregon City on October 20, 1847—a journey of 196 days across prairie and mountains that today we could cover in hours in a plane or a few days by car. The imagination soars at what the details of such a journey must have been. He stayed in Oregon his entire adult life, except for three years spent in the California gold fields. He married Jane Garwin in 1851. They produced nine children. A tragic streetcar accident in 1900 resulted in a ruptured blood vessel and the loss of his eyesight. His obituary praised him as a pioneer and a respected, prominent and valued citizen of Oregon.

Stephen's brother Cyrus Langworthy (1791–1874) joined the army, was promoted to lieutenant and fought in the War of 1812. He witnessed Master Commandant Oliver Hazard Perry's victory at the Battle of Lake Erie or Put-in-Bay on September 10, 1813. He and his wife, Charlotte, moved to Mansfield, Ohio, where he was involved in carding mills and banking. They then moved to Lexington, Ohio, where he established larger carding mills. Finally, they moved to Bureau County, Illinois, where he served as sheriff and became a member of the state legislature in 1842, according to the *History of Bureau County, Illinois*:

> *As Sheriff he had to bring in the new and sometimes wild elements of border life under the strong arm of the law. The rough lawbreakers at times made it necessary* [for the officer] *of the law to exercise the coolest courage in facing these men. Mr. Langworthy, except a lameness, was a man of remarkable physical strength and endurance and his courage was equal to this physical strength. He was crippled as a young man in this way. He was cutting down a tree and as it commenced to fall he noticed one of his small children playing just where it would fall. He rushed forward and gathered the child and threw it out of danger and saved it, but was caught himself, and his thigh was broken. It was never properly set, it seems, and made him lame through life.*

Benjamin Franklin Langworthy (1822–1907), Cyrus's son, attended school with William Tecumseh Sherman while living in Ohio. Later he moved to Princeton, Illinois, where he worked as an express driver delivering goods between St. Louis and Galena. He often carried supplies for Ulysses Grant, who lived and worked in Galena. Benjamin also knew Abraham Lincoln and frequently heard him conduct cases in court. From Illinois, he moved to Watertown, Wisconsin. He had to take a boat from Cleveland to Milwaukee, as there were no trains west of Buffalo. He established a mercantile business there and a second store in Oshkosh, Wisconsin, in 1846. He married Sarah Clemens in 1849. She was a cousin of the famous author Samuel Clemens, better known as Mark Twain. Benjamin and Sarah moved to Dubuque, Iowa, in 1854 to work with his cousins Edward, Lucius, James and Solon Langworthy in the banking business. Still filled with the urge to keep moving to the ever-expanding frontier, they settled in Chatfield, Minnesota. There he opened the land office of Langworthy and O'Farrell. Always interested in owning land, he filed a claim on eighty acres, eventually moving to the farm. He published the *Spring Valley Mercury* and edited it for twenty years before turning the newspaper over to his son Forrest. During the Civil War, Benjamin served as colonel of the Militia of Mower County. Benjamin was elected to the Minnesota State Constitutional Convention and the first legislature.

Lucius Lucene Langworthy (1837–1930), another of Cyrus's sons, lived in Massena, Iowa, where he farmed. Among the first to volunteer at the outbreak of the Civil War, Lucius was lieutenant of Company I in the 12th Illinois Volunteers. He served for the duration of the war. During his first tour of duty under General Ulysses S. Grant, Lucius saw combat at Fort Donelson and Shiloh. He then transferred to General William T. Sherman's ranks, where he participated in the March to the Sea. Covering the entire distance on foot, Lucius participated in several battles and the taking of Atlanta. After the war, on Christmas Eve 1865, he and Sarah Daniels married in Massena. They had seven children. A family history noted that for sixty years, no deaths occurred in their family—a fact worth noting in the days before vaccinations and antibiotics.

Benjamin Langworthy (1790–1864), Stephen's brother, accompanied the family to Hopkinton, New York, but then returned to Vermont, where he married Phebe Hamblin in 1827. They continued west to Lexington, Ohio, then Indian Loon, Illinois (near Chicago, probably Loon Lake), and finally in 1853 to St. Charles, Minnesota. Benjamin served during the War of 1812 at the Battle of Plattsburg, as did his brother Stephen. In Minnesota, he worked as a cabinetmaker and farmer.

Stephen C. Langworthy (1824–1904), son of Stephen and Jane Langworthy, married Elizabeth Bennett of New York in 1837. Their marriage produced six children. When his father, Dr. Stephen Langworthy, died in 1848, he supported his mother and younger siblings. To secure more funds, he traveled west to the gold fields of California in 1849. Rather than waste his time seeking the elusive gold, he took a more practical approach by selling supplies to the miners. He returned as a wealthy man. In 1858, he moved to Monticello, Iowa, where his mother lived. He opened mercantile, grain and lumber businesses there. He organized the Monticello National Bank and became its president. Fueled by the ever-present desire to move west, the family left Monticello for Seward, Nebraska. There he established the Seward County Bank, which merged into the First National Bank, and served as its president. Stephen C. Langworthy was also a veteran of the army during the Spanish-American War of 1898.

Franklin Langworthy (1798–1867), a brother of Stephen, studied in Potsdam, New York, for six months in 1828. Ordained a Universalist minister in 1829 in Clinton, New York, he moved west to Mount Carroll, Illinois. On April 1, 1850, he embarked on an overland journey to the gold fields of California just as his nephew did, but not for gold. Franklin sought knowledge, observations and the opportunity to teach. His return journey took him to New York via Panama (before the canal), followed by a rail journey back to Mount Carroll. He published *Scenery of the Plains, Mountains, and Mines; or a Diary Kept upon the Overland Route to California* in 1855. Princeton University republished the work in 1932, edited by Paul C. Phillips of the University of Montana under the new title *Narratives of the Trans-Mississippi Frontier*. Phillips said of Langworthy, "The author has an understanding of geology, botany and zoology. He believed the theory of evolution before Darwin published the *Origin of the Species*. He was an early advocate of the Trans Pacific railroad. While traveling he delivered lectures to his fellow travelers. His book is the only contemporary narrative that gives a philosophical description of the Overland Route to California in the days of the gold rush." Franklin Langworthy moved west again, this time to St. Charles, Minnesota, halfway between Rochester and Winona. There he served as a county supervisor in 1858. Benjamin Langworthy, his brother, wrote that "he has a good two story dwelling and a store. He has sold $1000.00 worth of his book and has $700 or $800 more to sell."

Stephen G. Williams (1827–1910), son of Laura Langworthy (sister of Stephen), headed west across the prairies and mountains seeking gold. He also decided that selling goods to the miners was a surer and easier way to prosperity than searching for gold. He established a successful mercantile business in Marysville, California. Stephen and Hannah Hendrickson married in 1855. Later, they moved to San Francisco, where they remained. Their marriage produced eight children.

Horace Greeley extolled these brave men and women who first "let the day-light into the woods" and expressed great satisfaction that such people could still be found in "the whaler in the Pacific, the packet-ship at Canton, the mining 'gulch' in California or the lead diggings of the Upper Mississippi."

By 1811, all of the Langworthy siblings were located in Hopkinton, New York, except James, Phineas and Laura. They did not remain stationary for very long. The restless pioneer spirit so evident in the eighteenth and nineteenth centuries had its firm grip on the Langworthy family.

THE MASSEY FAMILY

Massey Station, located nine miles south of Dubuque on a high bank overlooking the Mississippi River, once thrived as a clamming site, and it later developed into a popular recreational destination. We are left to wonder if the people harvesting clams or the vacationers reveling in the cool waters of the river recognized the origin of its place name, the importance of the Massey family or their connections to the Langworthys of Dubuque history.

Dubuque families developed Massey Station and nearby Shawondasee into resort areas along the Mississippi River to escape the city in the heat and humidity of the Iowa summer. Each family owned a cabin and the land that it occupied. Frank Noel built twelve summer cottages at Massey Station in 1897 to promote the area. Some of the cabins could also be rented on a weekly or monthly basis. Daily train service allowed easy access to and from Dubuque. School, business and church groups often traveled to Massey Station for picnics and social outings. On a sunny day in 1896, St. John's Lutheran Church of Dubuque left on the Eagle Point Ferry for an excursion to Bellevue, Iowa. A sudden, severe storm nearly sank the boat in the heavy waves. They struggled to make it into Massey Station and safety. One child fell overboard in the chaos but happily was rescued.

Ed Volkert—poet, author, naturalist and philosopher—wrote a whimsical publication known as the *Massey Miracle* detailing the comings and goings and "who done its" at Massey Station for years. He had worked as a printer for the *Telegraph Herald* newspaper, where he acquired the moniker "Sage of Massey." Another well-known resident, Herb Pfeffer, maintained a three-

Gate and path to Massey Station.

room cottage at Massey Station as an art studio. Pfeffer, a native of Dubuque, studied art out west and had lived at an art colony in Taos, New Mexico, for several years. He returned to Iowa to devote his time and talent to local scenes and people. His favorite painting was the *Massey One Room School*, with children playing around the pump. The art critics' favorite, however, was a portrait of Ed Volkert, his neighbor. One critic said that the painting was so realistic it seemed "Volker would spit tobacco juice at any second." Pfeffer had a wood stove for heat and retrieved water from a nearby stream. He thoroughly enjoyed the location and its inspiration. His one-man show at the University of Dubuque in 1949 received vigorous acclaim from the public.

An interesting note on the Masseys is that many members of the family worked for the railroads in the area. Clifford Massey wrote an article for the *Illinois Central Magazine* stating that his entire family worked for the railroad, including his maternal grandmother, who was in charge of the pumping station at Julien, Iowa, near Dubuque, when a horse and sweep (a horse-powered sweep was used to drive machinery) provided the only source of power. The only exception to the family's railroad career record was his sister Jeanette, who had not yet committed but did say that she "may be interested in railroad work sometime."

So, just who were these Massey family members, how were they connected to the Langworthy family and Dubuque and what were their stories?

Jonathon Massey (1747–1830) and Betty Woodbury (1748–1819) married in 1766. Both were born in Salem, New Hampshire, and died in Potsdam, New York. Betty's family figured prominently in early United States history as did the Langworthys. Her father, Jonathon Woodbury, and mother, Lydia Dodge, were married on June 24, 1735. Their family of eighteen or nineteen children included not only Betty but also Elisha Woodbury, who was born on December 29, 1735, in Massachusetts. He served as a captain in Colonel John Stark's regiment during the American Revolution. Both his father, Jonathon Woodbury, and his son Elisha Jr. served under his command. Jonathon died in 1776, but Elisha Jr. carried a bugle up Bunker Hill with his father, who commanded a company there. The bugle is now in the Beverly, Massachusetts Museum. Elisha Sr. also commanded a company at Ticonderoga, New York, and most famously at the Battle of Bennington. Colonel and later Brigadier General John Stark, a fellow New Hampshire resident, fought with the British in the French and Indian War. He was captured and adopted by the Abenaki nation and ransomed a year later for 103 Spanish dollars (approximately $3,000 today). When the British ordered Rogers' Rangers to attack an Abenaki village in Quebec in 1759, Stark refused, knowing that his adopted relatives might be there. He resigned his commission and returned to New Hampshire. The American Revolution created patriots of Stark and the Woodbury family. The Battle of Bennington, Vermont, on August 16, 1777, resulted in a defeat for the British and their Hessian allies. Since the British army remained relatively small, mercenary soldiers were necessary. Britain hired German soldiers from Hesse, in what is today Germany, to fight in the American Revolution. The colonial victory contributed to the British defeat at the Battle of Saratoga in October 1777. The Battle of Saratoga is regarded as a turning point toward a victory for the American colonies in the American Revolution, so its importance cannot be overstated.

Jonathon Massey also fought in the American Revolution as a sergeant in Captain Jeremiah Dow's Company, Colonel Welch's Regiment of volunteers, which joined the northern Continental army. Dow's Company in Colonel Welch's Regiment also participated in the American colonial victory at the Battle of Bennington. They then continued on to Saratoga, where they contributed to the defeat and surrender of General Burgoyne's British forces. So often these family members participated not only in the same war but also the same battles. Did they find one another? We can only speculate, but the question is intriguing.

Jonathon and Betty Woodbury Massey married in 1766. They later moved to Watertown, New York, where their graves are located. Their children included Daniel, Molly, Woodbury, Hart, Deborah, Jonathon, Isaiah, Betsey (Betty), Edward, Silas, Edward and Baker. Daniel Massey has a fascinating story. He married Rebeckah Kelly on August 30, 1787. They moved with a daughter and three sons to Ontario, Canada, in 1802 in search of cheaper land. They crossed Lake Ontario onboard a schooner, becoming some of the first settlers of Grafton, Ontario, then known as Grover's Tavern. By 1808, they owned land and livestock and lived in a log home with their increased family of three daughters and three sons. When the War of 1812 erupted, Daniel and his eldest two sons were called to serve in the Canadian military, fighting against their American cousins. Samuel, the eldest son, died in 1813, leaving Daniel Jr. in charge of the family and farm. He succeeded, but in 1817, at the age of only nineteen, he left home. Since legally he could not leave home until age twenty-one, he forfeited his inheritance.

Jonathon, the youngest of the sons, then inherited the family farm. He married Rachel Merrill in 1814 and bought 500 more acres to add to the original farm. Overcome with grief when their youngest son died at the age of six, they moved a few miles to the west and purchased 330 acres for a new farm. Jonathon died in 1832, with Rachel following in 1838. Tragedy struck when their son Jonathon was killed during a barn raising in 1834, leaving his son Samuel, at age seventeen, responsible for his mother and siblings—the youngest only twenty months. Samuel married Mary Masters in 1839. Their marriage produced seven children. Three of their daughters stayed in Canada, but the sons and one daughter moved to the United States. Samuel joined the Montreal Snow Shoe Club. Its members enjoyed weekly treks through the countryside on Sunday afternoons during the long Canadian winters, as well as races with other Canadian groups. In 1858, they built what became known as the "Ontario House." They named the Georgian-style home Sunnyside. It was an imposing structure with walls of locally quarried rose quartz. Mary died in 1890 and Samuel in 1899. The house was sold in 1907.

Meanwhile, Daniel (1789–1856) had accumulated one thousand acres in Ontario. Daniel imported a threshing machine and a power sweep to drive it in 1845. He started his own machine shop and foundry to manufacture power sweeps in about 1848. With his son Hart Massey, he founded the Massey Manufacturing Company. The company expanded into the Massey-Harris Company and finally the Massey-Ferguson Company, manufacturing agricultural equipment. The family became one of the leading families of Ontario. In 1882, Hart Massey purchased a mansion built by Lord William

Massey-Harris exhibit. *Langworthy scrapbook, Center for Dubuque History, Loras College.*

Massey Mansion, Toronto, Canada. *Langworthy scrapbook, Center for Dubuque History, Loras College.*

Massey Family Mausoleum, Mount Pleasant Cemetery, Toronto, Canada. *Wikimedia Commons.*

McMaster, who founded McMaster College of Hamilton, Ontario. The home, with twenty-six rooms and seventeen fireplaces, was built in 1867. The Masseys added a turret, a veranda and a greenhouse. Other Massey family members built homes in the surrounding area, not unlike their Langworthy cousins in Dubuque. To the north, Hart Massey's son Chester built their family home, where his sons, Vincent and Raymond, were raised. Raymond Massey became a famous actor in American films and television. In 1915, with commercial enterprises imposing on their neighborhood, the family left the home and bequeathed it to Victoria College. When Hart Massey died in 1896, he decreed that the majority of his estate be disposed of by 1916 to the benefit of public institutions and causes. As a result, the Massey Foundation was created to ensure that their philanthropy touched nearly every segment of Toronto life. In 1959, the Massey Medal was established to recognize "outstanding personal achievement in exploration, development or description of geography of Canada." The medal is awarded annually by the Royal Canadian Geographical Society.

Another son of Jonathon and Betty Massey, Isaiah Massey (1778–1820), became a physician following in the footsteps of his uncle, Dr. Woodbury

Hart Massey portrait. *Wikimedia Commons.*

Massey of Salem, New Hampshire, who was an army surgeon during the War of 1812. Isaiah arrived in Watertown, New York, in 1801 and opened the first medical office there. He donated land in 1805 for the town public square. In 1806, he founded the Jefferson County Medical Society and served as its first treasurer. Massey Street in Watertown remains as a tribute to his standing in the community.

Stephen and Betsey Massey Langworthy moved to Hopkinton, New York, where he practiced medicine. He also was a U.S. marshal for the northern district of New York and collected revenues for the New York Customs House. The siren call of the frontier was impossible to ignore for many Americans, including Stephen and Betsey Massey Langworthy. They immigrated to Erie, Pennsylvania, in 1815. There they established a sawmill, but the desire to go west overtook them again in 1818. After loading their belongings and twelve children on a flatboat, they set off down French Creek to the Allegheny River to the Ohio River. The adventures and hardships of a wilderness lay before them.

WESTWARD HO!

*W*hile descending the Ohio River, misfortune struck at Letarts Falls for Stephen and Betsey Langworthy and their family. These falls no longer exist due to dam construction, but Lewis and Clark noted that in 250 feet the water level dropped 4 feet. The Langworthy family lost all their belongings and nearly their lives attempting to navigate these rough waters. They stopped at Marietta, Ohio, until spring, when a new mode of transportation could be found.

In the following spring, at Shawneetown, Illinois, they sold their flatboat to purchase horses and wagons. Old Shawneetown had been established as a village in 1748 by the Pekowi Shawnee. Lewis and Clark had traveled through the village in 1803 on their way to Fort Massac on the Ohio River. After the American Revolution, Shawneetown became an important U.S. administrative center for the Northwest Territory. Stephen Langworthy once served as a government administrative official for the Northwest Territory. Washington, D.C., and Shawneetown are the only towns to have been chartered by the U.S. government rather than a state or local municipality. Unfortunately, in 1937, a devastating flood destroyed the town, and most residents moved to higher ground.

The Langworthys continued their journey to Edwardsville, Illinois (about thirty miles from St. Louis). Here in 1819, they bought a farm for the family to operate while Dr. Langworthy practiced medicine in St. Louis. Tragedy struck the family when Betsey and son Stephen succumbed to malaria in April 1820. Eldest son, James, and his uncle, Dr. Isaiah Massey (Betsey's brother),

James Lyon Langworthy. *Center for Dubuque History, Loras College.*

traveled northwest to find a healthier place to live. They settled on Diamond Grove, Illinois, and built a log cabin. Dr. Massey and his children—Woodbury, Benjamin, Henry and Louisa—had moved to Edwardsville with the Langworthys. James and Dr. Massey intended to farm the land at Diamond Grove that had been previously cultivated by the Kickapoo Indians. Dr. Massey returned to Edwardsville to inform the family of their upcoming move. There he died of malaria, leaving his family with the Langworthys.

Malaria is a disease caused by a parasite spread to humans through the bites of infected mosquitoes. While no longer common in the United States, it was a problem for settlers on the frontier living in low-lying areas near stagnant water.

Dr. Stephen Langworthy returned to St. Louis after his family moved to Diamond Grove and began to farm their new land. He met and married Jane Berthinia Moureing, originally from South Carolina, who was twenty-six years younger than he. The Moureing family had moved to St. Charles, Missouri, in 1815. Stephen and Jane eventually had nine more children: Stephen, William, Cyrus (1830–1833), Elizabeth, Cella, Oella Pauline, Charlotte, Pliny and Cyrus (it was not unusual to name subsequent children after deceased siblings). Both his medical practice and the farm prospered.

Meanwhile, eldest son, James (1800–1865)—who was described as a black-haired, black-eyed, fine-looking gentleman—heard rumors of the wealth available in the Upper Mississippi River Lead Mining District centered on Galena, Illinois, and Hardscrabble (Hazel Green), Wisconsin. In 1824, he rode north on horseback to investigate the rumors. After ten days riding across the wilderness, Smith arrived in Galena, a village of four or five houses. James Langworthy and Orrin Smith of Cincinnati, Ohio, began mining lead near Hardscrabble. The name Hardscrabble reflected "the terrible encounters that took place between contending parties for possession of a lode, in which hard blows, rifles and bowie knives were freely used." Smith arrived in Galena as a fifteen-year-old in 1823 with Dr. Moses Meeker. Meeker had traveled from New York to Cincinnati to Galena. He obtained a mineral land lease from Secretary

CROSS SECTION OF A LEAD MINE
From the Report of David Dale Owen, 1839

Lead mine sketch, David Dale Owens, 1839. *Wisconsin Room, University of Wisconsin–Platteville.*

of War J.C. Calhoun. In 1823, he arrived in Galena with his family and workers after investigating the region a year earlier. He began successful mining and smelting businesses immediately.

After two years, James and Orrin struck lead and sold their claim to Alexander Phelps in 1826. They made a $20,000 profit. The money for the claim and the profits from the lead allowed James to return to Diamond Grove to visit his family. Smith also used his profits for a return visit to his home in Cincinnati. Having confirmed the rumors of lead riches, James returned to Wisconsin and mining with Smith. Other members of the Langworthy family envisioned new lives in the Lead District. In 1827, Lucius, Edward, Mary Ann and Maria Langworthy traveled by wagon driven by Solon Langworthy to "Woods Woodyard" (Quincy, Illinois). They arrived on April 10 and boarded the steamboat *Red Rover*. Solon, however, turned the wagon around and headed home. Sadly, a bull killed one of his horses, so he abandoned the wagon and rode the remaining horse to Diamond Grove.

The Langworthy siblings joined James and Orrin Smith at Buncombe after arriving in Galena via steamboat. Buncombe was a mining settlement near the Wisconsin and Illinois border. Mary Ann Langworthy and Orrin Smith married in 1827. Smith became the sheriff in Galena in 1830. Prior to steamboats, the voyageurs, who had transported their furs in pirogues (a boat similar to a mix between a canoe and a keelboat) over shallow waters and rapid streams, used poles and oars to proceed up and down the Mississippi River. While later travelers enjoyed the relative luxury of a steamboat, the voyageurs slept on sandbars or anchored out in the river to avoid mosquitoes, thieves and hostile natives and lived on salt pork and dry biscuit. They covered barely eight miles a day. A journey from Quincy, Illinois, to Galena required thirty days. On board a steamboat, a trip from Galena to St. Paul took two days and sixteen hours. In 1836, the steamboat *Missouri Fulton* made the trip between Dubuque and St. Louis in seventy-eight hours. Travel overland remained nearly impossible, as few roads existed and those that did were often impassable due to mud, ice and snow or flooding.

Lucius (1807–1865) and Edward Langworthy (1808–1893) moved to Coon Branch near Hazel Green (Hardscrabble), built a cabin and began mining. Mary Ann had married Orrin Smith, so Maria stayed with her sister and brother-in-law. James Langworthy maintained friendly relationships with the Sac and Mesquakie (Fox), who lived in the region. They even allowed him to visit their village at the mouth of Catfish Creek. The Indians had steadfastly denied any American or European visitors at this site since the death of Julien Dubuque in 1810. This early knowledge of the geography and resources of the region became invaluable to the Langworthy family once Iowa opened to settlement.

Solon (1814–1886) and his brother Lucius had farmed one hundred acres at Diamond Grove. Despite heavy yields, their profits were minuscule. As an example, they exchanged one thousand bushels of corn for a $100 horse. Eliza Langworthy married William Maclay, and Laura Langworthy married Jacob Williams in 1827. With his sisters' marriages and the miserable profits on the farm, Solon decided to leave for greener pastures in the Lead District. Along with Horace McCartney, he left for Galena in April 1828. They encountered a group of Indians, who traveled with them to the Rock River. Despite warnings, they had no trouble, even engaging in wrestling matches with the young Indian men. Once they swam their horses across the Rock River, they continued on to Council Hill, Illinois, where the companions separated. Solon continued to Buncombe to meet James. Solon, Edward, Lucius and James were reunited at the mining site of Coon Branch in Wisconsin. Solon then accompanied his brother-in-law, Orrin Smith, to British Hollow on the Platte River in Wisconsin for a much-anticipated visit with his sisters Mary Ann and Maria.

Solon resided with Lucius and Edward while they mined at Coon Branch. Their efforts proved so successful that Solon used his profits to return to Diamond Grove in November 1828 with a friend, James Meredith. Solon remained working on the farm for the next three years.

In 1829, James Langworthy explored the area west of the Mississippi River from the Maquoketa River to the Turkey River with permission of the Sac and Mesquakie. He had Indian guides to assist him and ensure that he was not mining. In 1830, Mesquakie and Sac chiefs from the Little Fox Village on Catfish Creek at the Dubuque Mines were traveling to Prairie du Chien for a conference to address constant warfare among the various native groups. Near the present site of Cassville, Wisconsin, a group of Dakota attacked their canoes. Only one man survived to tell the story. As a result, the Mesquakie and Sac left the Dubuque Mines. James Langworthy and others quickly crossed the Mississippi River in canoes, with their horses swimming beside them. They described a large village of seventy buildings constructed of poles and tree bark, with a council house whose inner sides were covered in paintings representing buffalo, elk, bear, panther, sports and war—all was deserted. According to legend, the bluff just to the south of the village has been haunted by a youthful fairy form that comes to the site where Dakota warriors killed and threw the bodies of Sac and Mesquakie warriors off the cliff during their last battle there. The new arrivals noted that bones were still visible at the bottom of the cliff. Tragically, vandals destroyed the village, denying any future knowledge of its structure or history.

The miners also saw cornfields stretching up the hillsides and ravines. Circular, linear and square mounds dotted the area. Burials had occurred in these mounds, but also bodies wrapped in blankets and placed on tree limbs along where Main Street is now located were visible. Grave robbers disturbed the burials, stealing articles buried with the dead. Grotesquely, even the teeth of the dead were stolen to be sold for false teeth. According to Lucius Langworthy, the miners stopped the grave robbers. Farther to the north, they witnessed one thousand acres of tall grass, corn stalks and level land running up to the shore of the Mississippi River. This area, known as Couler Valley, soon became the center of the Langworthy lead claim. James, Lucius and others began mining illegally at the site. The Langworthy brothers lived in a cabin of their own construction near their mine. It was described as being built into the hillside, with a wall of loose stone about four feet high. The opposite end and one side were fashioned of posts, with brush filling in the open spaces. The fourth side was left open. The roof consisted of brush and slabs of wood. The soil of the lead region was once considered sterile and not fit for farming. Happily, that assertion proved false, but it meant that the early miners believed they needed to import food supplies.

Soldiers commanded by Lieutenant Jefferson Davis (future president of the Confederacy) stationed at Prairie du Chien often patrolled the region and expelled the miners, who then fled to islands in the Mississippi River or to the eastern banks in Illinois and Wisconsin. As soon as the soldiers departed, the miners returned.

The story of Jefferson Davis at the DuBuque Mines (Dubuque) is an intriguing one, as if cut from the pages of a romantic novel. In 1828, Lieutenant Jefferson Davis boarded a steamboat in his home state of Mississippi bound for Jefferson Barracks at St. Louis, from where he was assigned to Fort Crawford at Prairie du Chien. He helped to cut logs along Red Cedar River in northern Wisconsin and float them down the Chippewa River to the Mississippi River for their destination at Prairie du Chien in order to build the fortifications there for Fort Crawford. This was a very dangerous assignment given the hostilities of the Indians, the danger of cutting trees and the hazardous task of log rafting on rivers swollen by spring floods.

Meanwhile, in 1829, Lieutenant Colonel Zachary Taylor along with his wife, son and three daughters arrived in Prairie du Chien for his assignment commanding Fort Crawford. In 1831, Lieutenant Davis returned to Prairie du Chien and no doubt was charmed by Taylor's beautiful daughter, Sarah. She returned the affection, as the couple courted in the presence of her father. This idyllic scene soon changed.

During a court-martial at Fort Crawford, Davis, Major Thomas Smith and another young officer served as the court, with Taylor acting as president of the court-martial trial. The accused young officer appeared at the proceedings absent his uniform, which he claimed had been delayed in St. Louis. Taylor, a stickler for regulations, berated him severely and refused to continue the court-martial. Finally, a vote was called, and Davis voted with Smith, overruling Taylor. An angry discussion resulted in Taylor swearing at Davis, prohibiting him to even enter the Taylor home and forbidding his marriage to Sarah.

To ensure that Sarah and Davis were kept apart, Taylor sent Lieutenant Davis south to the Lead Mine District to expel the miners who were on Indian Territory illegally. Undoubtedly, Taylor thought that the miners— who believed the American government was denying them their rightful access to the rich lead veins—would kill Davis and eliminate his problem.

Because the Dubuque lead mines were on the west bank of the Mississippi River, they were on Indian lands. Since Julien Dubuque's death in 1810, the Mesquakie and Sac had destroyed all the buildings and furiously protected the region. Galena and Mineral Point to the east had become the centers of the lead rush in the Driftless Region (so named due to the absence of glaciation during the last glacial period). The miners often crossed the river to mine illegally.

Lieutenant Davis had a reputation as an excellent negotiator, so rather than attack the miners, he met with them in a drinking establishment at the DuBuque Mines. The fact that there was a "drinking establishment" at the mines indicated just how many miners had arrived. He persuaded the miners to leave, burned the cabins and returned to Fort Crawford. Once the military had vacated the mines, the miners returned. It was a familiar dance. Prospects for the permanent ownership of the mines by the Indians were dim.

Sarah Taylor and Lieutenant Davis vowed to marry despite her father's opposition. In June 1835, Lieutenant Jefferson Davis quit the military and followed Sarah to her aunt's plantation in Kentucky, where they were wed on June 17, 1835.

So, once again, after the soldiers exited the area, the miners returned. In June 1830, James Langworthy, H.F. Lander, James McPheeters, Samuel H. Scoles and E.M. Urn signed the Miners' Compact:

We, a committee having been chosen to draft certain rules and regulations, by which we, as miners, will be governed; and, having duly considered the subject, do unanimously agree that we will be governed by the regulations on the east side of the Mississippi River with the following exceptions, to wit: Article I. That each and every man shall hold 200 yards square of ground by working said ground one day in six. Article II. We further agree, that there shall be chosen by the majority of the miners present, a person who shall hold this article, and who shall grant letters of arbitration, on application being made, and that said letter arbitration shall be obligatory on the parties concerned so applying. To the above, we the undersigned subscribe.

The Miners' Compact has been considered the first set of laws in what became Iowa.

The soldiers returned in 1830 to drive the miners out of the region. James and Lucius fled to an island in the Mississippi River, returning to spend the winter in a tent next to their lead. When the Indians returned to their rightful land after hostilities with the Dakota ceased, the miners were forced to watch from the islands as the "fruits of our industry and enterprise were consumed." The flood of Americans into the Lead District east of the Mississippi River exerted tremendous pressure on opening the lands west of the river that up to this time had remained Indian Territory. Soldiers again arrived at the mines in 1832, under the command of Lieutenant J.B. Gardenier, to expel the illegal miners. The outbreak of the Black Hawk War caused the soldiers to return to their units. James Langworthy and Thomas Kelly returned to the Dubuque Mines and petitioned the secretary of war for permission to mine the lead. They were ordered to leave by Marmaduke S. Davenport, the Indian agent at Fort Armstrong (Davenport, Iowa). Soldiers arrived under the command of Lieutenant George Wilson to drive out the miners but allowed them to stay since the Mesquakie had left the area. When Davenport heard this in February 1833, he investigated and found the miners had been joined by some St. Louis claimants to the Spanish Grant of Julien Dubuque. Once again, soldiers, who marched down to the Dubuque Mines from Prairie du Chien on the Mississippi River ice, drove out the miners. Carrying what lead they could, the miners occupied the islands in the river. They did not have to wait long.

In the mid-1700s, the Sac and Mesquakie established the village of Saukenuk at the confluence of the Rock and Mississippi Rivers. The presence of burial mounds indicated that the site had been home to various

Black Hawk. George
Catlin portrait.
Wikimedia Commons.

peoples for hundreds of years. The fields were fertile, game was plentiful and lead mining to the north was profitable.

In 1767, Makataimeshekiakiak, or Black Sparrow, was born. As a young man, he wore the feathers and skin of the Sparrow Hawk around his waist to gain the power of this bird of prey. However, a series of events had already begun that would bring him fame, end a way of life for an entire people, increase the status and wealth of families such as the Langworthys and allow new cities to grow—Dubuque among them.

During the colonial and revolutionary era, the Sac and Mesquakie supported the British due to an extensive trade network between them. An American force even attacked and burned Saukenuk during the Revolution to weaken the British. After the American Revolution, the Sac and Mesquakie found themselves in the Northwest Territory of the United States with no assistance or guarantees from their former allies, the British. With few settlers in the wilderness, the Indians noticed little change.

The year 1803 brought sweeping changes. Spain had secretly transferred Louisiana to France, and Napoleon had grand schemes of empire that failed to materialize. Americans feared losing the use of the Mississippi River and its valuable port of New Orleans to some European power. As a result, in the Louisiana Purchase, President Jefferson bought not only New Orleans but also a vast territory stretching from the Mississippi River to the Rocky Mountains. He then sent Lewis and Clark to explore, map and establish contact with the Indians in this new region for the purpose of trade.

Americans who arrived in St. Louis assumed ownership of the upper territory, including the Mines of Spain at the DuBuque Mines (Dubuque). Soon thousands of settlers moved into Illinois and Wisconsin, demanding the lead lands in Iowa.

In 1804, a settler was killed by a Sac warrior. Four Sac men escorted the guilty warrior to St. Louis with trade goods as compensation to the dead man's family. According to Sac law, they could all then return to their village. A federal investigation did result in a pardon, but before the document reached St. Louis from Washington, D.C., the Sac warrior was shot and killed trying to escape. The council held to settle the murder case had ulterior motives. President Jefferson believed that Indians should assimilate into an agricultural lifestyle. Those who refused could move west of the Mississippi, where civilization—he wrongly predicted—would take hundreds of years to reach. Adding to the tempest, the British suggested that they would assist the Indians against the Americans. William Henry Harrison, territorial governor of Indiana and future president of the United States, conducted the treaty negotiations at this council with the four Sac men who had traveled to St. Louis to settle the murder. They were not chiefs, had no understanding of treaties or landownership and had no approval from their tribe to negotiate beyond the murder; however, they affixed their marks to the Treaty of 1804 ceding all Sac land east of the Mississippi River.

The War of 1812 complicated matters when Black Hawk and his warriors, with the help of the British, drove Major Zachary Taylor and 430 soldiers off Credit Island at the mouth of the Rock River. Despite this and other victories the Indians were abandoned by the British again when they signed the Treaty of Ghent and ended the War of 1812.

The lead rush of the 1820s heightened the demand for Indian land in Illinois, Wisconsin and at the DuBuque Mines. Meanwhile, in Saukenuk, farmers had arrived from the East. In 1828, based on the Treaty of 1804, the Sac and Mesquakie were instructed to leave their villages within one year. When they left for their winter hunting grounds that winter, it was expected they would never return across the Mississippi River. Black Hawk defiantly decided to return to his village in the spring of 1829, only to find it occupied by settlers. Conflict was inevitable.

When Andrew Jackson became president in March 1829, he represented a Democrat Party that had won on the basis of his Indian fighter reputation and promise of lands for the settlers. He believed that all Indians had to be removed west of the Mississippi River. Black Hawk became more defiant.

In the spring of 1831, while Keokuk's band (Sac and Mesquakie) remained in Iowa, Black Hawk and 300 warriors plus women and children returned to Saukenuk. On June 25, 1831, 1,500 militiamen arrived with orders to attack Saukenuk. They were frustrated to find that Black Hawk had secretly abandoned the village and returned to Iowa during the night. Encouraged by promised support from other tribes and the British, Black Hawk's band increased to 2,000 in the spring of 1832. They intended to return to their village. Andrew Jackson faced reelection in 1832. The settlers who had supported him demanded land. The American Indians had to go.

On April 5, Black Hawk's band crossed the Mississippi River. It is hard to imagine when driving down Ninth Street in Rock Island today that all the country focused its attention on this spot in the spring of 1832.

Henry Gratiot, sub-agent for the Ho-Chunk nation (formerly known as the Winnebago), arrived to negotiate on April 23, but Black Hawk had moved to Dixon's Ferry, Illinois. He began to realize that the promised help from the British and other tribes was a false hope. Governor Reynolds of Illinois had ordered Major Isaiah Stillman's company of 250 militiamen to force Black Hawk to abandon his plans. When three unarmed Indians under a white flag approached, the drunken militia attacked, killing one of the unarmed men and two of the Indians watching from a nearby hill. Black Hawk and forty warriors rode toward the militia at a full gallop. The militia, except Captain John Adams and twelve men, panicked. While the others fled, Adams and his men fought to the death. The Indians unexpectedly won the Battle of Stillman's Run.

Rumor and gossip filled the countryside. Terrified people fled to forts and hastily built defenses. Black Hawk sought to cross into Iowa. On June 24, an attack on Muscohocoynak or Apple River, where a mining settlement had built a fort, resulted in the death of one settler and the naming of the village Elizabeth after the courageous Elizabeth Armstrong, who rallied the residents and stopped the Indians from taking the fort.

On July 21, Black Hawk reached the Wisconsin River. The Michigan Territory militia had caught up with him, so while most of the warriors helped others cross the river, forty to fifty warriors battled the troops from superior positions on the hilltops. The Battle of Wisconsin Heights was the longest and largest of the Black Hawk War. When the militia attacked, the Indians abandoned the hills for the swamps and riverbank, where many were killed. After dark, the Indians crossed the river. The soldiers remained in pursuit. Soldiers Grove, Wisconsin, was named for one of the army's encampments.

On August 1, the Indians reached the Mississippi River south of the Bad Axe River. Only 500 of the original 2,000 remained alive. While the Indians prepared to cross the river, the steamboat *Warrior* opened fire despite Black Hawk's attempt to surrender. As they were caught between the river and General Atkinson and General Henry's troops, the casualties were high. Many women and children were killed as they attempted to swim the river. The battle ended about noon. The Dakota, who had volunteered 150 warriors to fight against the "British Band"—as Black Hawk and his followers were known—arrived too late for the Battle of Bad Axe. They attacked the remnants of survivors on the Cedar River in Iowa; they killed 68 and took 22 prisoners. The Ho-Chunk also hunted the survivors of the British Band. They ultimately took fifty or sixty scalps. Between 150 and 200 Indians survived, while 7 Americans died in the Battle of Bad Axe. Black Hawk escaped to Prairie La Crosse, where he informed a Ho-Chunk village of his desire to surrender. They brought him to Prairie du Chien. On August 27, 1832, he surrendered to Joseph Street, the U.S. Indian agent at Fort Crawford.

General Dodge sent Henry L. Massey (Langworthy cousin) and James Langworthy to Rock Island to announce Black Hawk's defeat at Bad Axe. Lucius and Edward Langworthy both served in the military during the Black Hawk War. Lucius was a lieutenant at the Battle of Bad Axe. Solon Langworthy enlisted in Company A, U.S. Ranging Service, under Captain Nathaniel Boone (grandson of Daniel Boone) in July 1832. Solon was present at the treaty signing at Rock Island, Illinois, then stationed at Fort Gibson, a strategic site where the Arkansas, Verdigris and Grant Rivers converge in what is today Oklahoma. The Santa Fe Trail and the Texas Road located near here were important trade routes protected from Fort Gibson. In 1832, Fort Gibson became a semi-permanent outpost meant to deal with hostilities between the Osage nation, who had been there since the seventeenth century, and other Plains Indians. During the Indian Removal of the 1830s, Fort Gibson was the largest fort in the nation when the Cherokee nation was moved to Oklahoma along the Trail of

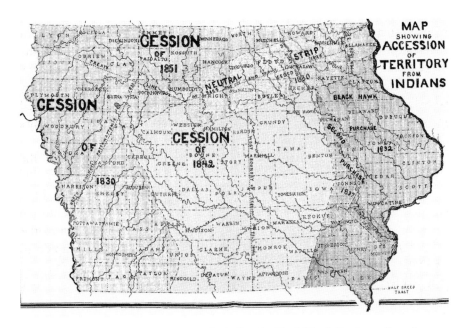

Map of Iowa after the Black Hawk War, including the Black Hawk Purchase. *Center for Dubuque History, Loras College.*

Tears. Washington Irving accompanied the troops led by Colonel Henry Dodge (after the death of General Leavenworth) to Fort Gibson in 1834. He wrote *A Tour of the Prairies* based on his observations and experiences there. Other famous Americans to serve at Fort Gibson during the early 1830s included Zachary Taylor, Stephen Kearny, Nathaniel Boone and Robert E. Lee.

Due to a cholera epidemic at Fort Armstrong (Rock Island, Illinois), Black Hawk was taken to Jefferson Barracks in Lemay, Missouri, just south of St. Louis to witness the Black Hawk Treaty. The United States purchased 6 million acres called the Iowa District. The Indians received $20,000 per year for thirty years, had their debts paid and received a blacksmith and gunsmith for their new settlements. Chief Keokuk was the official representative of the tribes. He presented several acres to Marguerite Le Claire, who was the granddaughter of a chief and the wife of Antoine Le Claire. Three years later, Davenport was plotted.

Black Hawk was taken on a tour of major American cities along with Keokuk and Colonel George Davenport. This common practice underscored the futility of further resistance. Black Hawk, his wife and their sons settled on the Des Moines River. He received visitors and was a guest speaker for many events. On October 3, 1838, he died at the age of seventy-one and was buried on the banks of the Des Moines River in Davis County.

As a result of the Black Hawk Purchase, on June 1, 1833, settlers and miners legally crossed the Mississippi River to stake claim to the lead lands and rich farmland located there. Although surrounded by uncharted territory, the city of Dubuque was officially chartered that same year. A new chapter had begun.

LEAD RUSH

John Sheldon arrived with a commission from Washington, D.C., as the U.S. agent for the Dubuque lead mine area. It was his unhappy job to regulate the miners and smelters. It is interesting to note that when President Zachary Taylor was interviewed about his tenure at Prairie du Chien trying to control illegal mining, he stated emphatically that the miners were worse than anything he had experienced in either the Seminole War in Florida or the Mexican-American War. Sheldon fared no better. The government expected the miners to pay and wait for permits and the smelters to buy licenses to operate. Since the miners and smelters believed they were doing the government's job of penetrating the wilderness for future societies and eventually states, they resisted all regulation. Sheldon left after one fruitless year. He accepted the important job as register of the Mineral Point, Wisconsin federal land office in 1834. Accused of misusing his position by favoring friends and colleagues when registering land deeds, he was dismissed. He moved to Madison and helped to found the *Madison Democrat* in 1843. He retired to his farm in Willow Springs, Lafayette County, Wisconsin, in 1860 after serving as a clerk in the Treasury Department in Washington, D.C.

In 1842, the U.S. government adopted a system of leasing mines and smelting furnaces. However, the citizens once more refused to recognize the right of the government to raise revenue from the hard work of the new settlers. John Flanegan arrived as the superintendent of mines in Wisconsin, Illinois and Iowa. He arrested the miners and smelters as trespassers and sent them to trial, where the jury levied a fine for each defendant of only five cents. Unable to continue enforcing the laws, the government opened the region to land sales in 1846.

James, Edward and Lucius Langworthy were already established in Dubuque. They and others who had arrived prior to the legal opening of the region had plotted the best sites for mines and other business endeavors. A colleague of the Langworthys who also arrived at the Dubuque Mines illegally, Thomas McCraney, played an important role in the development of the new territory along with the Langworthys. McCraney, born in New York in 1791, served in the War of 1812 at Fort George, New York, under Captain Samuel Ingersoll in the Seventh Regiment. He married Susan (Susanna) Slayton in 1814. Struck by the promise of riches in the lead county, they moved west. He arrived at the Dubuque Mines with James Langworthy. His family took up residence in a cabin in Jo Daviess County, Illinois, across the river from the Dubuque Mines. Dodging the soldiers, he built two cabins at what became known as McCraneys' Hollow (Eighth Street today). McCraney also built a smelting furnace and a cabin for his workers. He abandoned the cabin in Illinois and moved his family into one of the new cabins. When the soldiers returned in the winter of 1832, the miners fled to the islands while the soldiers burned the structures. With his wife expecting the birth of their seventh child any day, McCraney stealthily returned to the Dubuque Mines with his family to occupy a cabin the soldiers had missed. There, on January 10, 1833, Susan Ann McCraney was born—the first nonnative child born in Dubuque, Iowa.

When the Wisconsin Territory was organized, it included Iowa. McCraney represented Dubuque along with John Foley and Thomas McKnight at the First Territorial Legislature in Belmont, Wisconsin. The legislature created the Miners' Bank of Dubuque as the first bank in Iowa. The bank was required to have $200,000 of capital stock divided into shares of $100 each. The directors of the Miners' Bank were Ezekiel Lockwood, Francis Gehon,

Susan McCraney, daughter of Thomas and Susanna McCraney. *Encyclopedia Dubuque.*

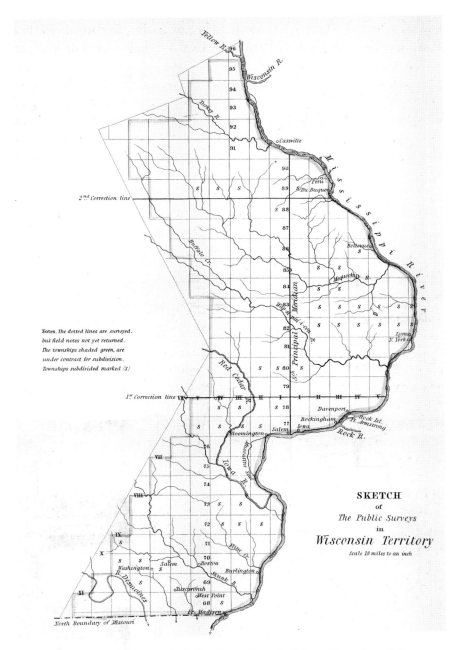

Map of the Wisconsin Territory, including Iowa. *Center for Dubuque History, Loras College.*

John Kirk, William Myers, Robert Sherman, William Carrill, Simeon Clark, E.M. Bissell and Lucius Langworthy.

Thomas and Susanna McCraney divorced in 1841. He then married Mary Ann Harwood Hill amid scandal and rumor. She was the widow of Dr. Allen Hill and the mother-in-law of Thomas McCraney's son, Orlando. Thomas and Mary Ann moved to Garnavillo, Iowa, in Clayton County. Upon the death of Thomas, Susanna McCraney sued Mary Ann McCraney for the estate. She claimed that the divorce was fraudulent and should be set aside. She won the suit and received one-third of the estate. When she died in 1868, her obituary read, "She was respected by all though domestic troubles were many and heavy upon her. She bore them with Christian fortitude."

Bessie V. McCraney, the great-great-granddaughter of Thomas and Susanna McCraney, taught school in Dubuque for fifty-two years. She was a director/principal at Lincoln and Audubon schools and a teacher at Franklin and Irving schools. She graduated from high school in 1917, obtained her teacher's certificate after passing the state teacher's exam and began teaching for twenty-five dollars per month. Her desk was a kitchen table with a drawer. "I was lucky to get [it] open." Of her teaching career, she stated, "I have very deep and wonderful feelings for the children I have taught. I hope they are happy. If they are happy, they are successful. I have never taught a child I didn't love."

On January 31, 1830, Edward and James Langworthy went west with two companions to the DuBuque Mines despite its illegality. When they got to Dunleith (East Dubuque), they found the river open, so they traveled north across from the confluence of the Little Maquoketa River. There the ice had not gone out, so they could move from one island to another toward the Iowa shore. At one point, they came to a space of open water twelve feet across. They bridged the divide with willow poles and continued their trek. On the western bank, they camped near Zollicoffer Lake. (The lake, on property owned by Jacob Zollicoffer, occupied the backwaters of the Mississippi River. It was one and a half miles long and three-fourths of a mile wide. Visitors later arrived at the popular picnic and ice harvesting site by train or steamboat. The lake no longer exists, as it was flooded when the Zebulon Pike Lock and Dam no. 11 were completed in 1937.) While camped at the water's edge, they built a large fire; Edward and James moved away from the fire and covered themselves in blankets. Their two companions stayed close to the fire but awakened to find themselves soaked due to wet snow that had fallen during the night. Edward and James, however, were warm under a foot of unmelted snow. When local natives who had been observing them all night told them to leave, they left.

In the fall of 1832, the Langworthys and three hundred miners returned to the DuBuque Mines. James Langworthy built a log cabin where Heeb's Brewery was later built (Central Avenue and East Twenty-Second Street), but it was destroyed when the soldiers returned. From 1835 to 1836, he added rail fencing, with a house set back from the property line (near Francis Street). Destroyed by a tornado, the house was rebuilt in a "more substantial manner." The farm became known as Tivoli Gardens. The Gardens later became Dubuque's first beer garden, operated by John Schaffner. In 1860, Dubuque's first Agricultural Fair was held at the Tivoli Gardens, with more than five hundred exhibits.

The Langworthy family, and other early arrivals such as the McCraneys, prospered due to their lead interests and land sales. The lead in Dubuque lay in large caverns either attached to the rocks or embedded in the clay and ocher that filled the crevices. Ocher is a pigment containing ferrous oxide and is yellow to red in color. According to Lucius Langworthy, both families hired workmen who, along with the owners, mined the Langworthy Lode. They carried a lamp or candle through very narrow spaces and found a subterranean vault completely filled with ore. He said that when illuminated, it resembled diamonds. The ore lay in great masses or was attached to the sides and roof in huge cubes. The miners yelled, "He has struck a cave!" when they located a vein of lead. The combined Langworthy, Thomas Kelly and Cardiff grounds amounted to 10 million pounds of lead. The veins of lead in Dubuque ran east–west under cap rock of variable thickness depending on the elevation of the mine. Along with Langworthy, rich lodes were also found by Thomas Leven. Other successful mines included the Bartlett and Stewart lodes, the Karrick mines and the McKenzie mines. While the lead mines brought prosperity to many, it became more and more difficult to remove from the earth. At about one hundred feet in depth, the miners hit water. Since the water table is relatively high near the Mississippi River, expensive equipment was needed to pump the water out before mining could continue. This additional expense meant that the days of the independent miner were numbered.

Lucius Hart Langworthy. *Center for Dubuque History, Loras College.*

43

In May 1834, a meeting of early settlers gathered across from the Lorimier and Gratiot store. About five hundred people were living at the DuBuque Mines by that time. A survey done in 1833 found that Main Street was a muddy track lined with stores, saloons and cabins. The settlers determined that the settlement needed a proper name. They decided against Washington as the name of their new town and instead settled on Dubuque, as it had already been known as the DuBuque Mines.

Solon Langworthy purchased a mineral lot on the Little Maquoketa River north of Dubuque at the Timber Diggings from Calvin Roberts for $1,000 in 1834. Roberts had worked the claim unsuccessfully. With Lucius, Solon struck a rich vein of lead, built a cabin at an unknown location and made a huge profit.

Solon Massey Langworthy. *Center for Dubuque History, Loras College.*

While Lucius returned to the city, Solon hired two men and worked the mine for a year and a half. The Timber Diggings or Ewing Range was also later known as Durango. It is located several miles north of the present site of Durango, Iowa. At one time, as many as 150 men worked at this mine. It is located where the northern section of Couler Valley meets the hills and bluffs along the Little Maquoketa River. There a series of crevices was mined for a length of two miles. These crevices or fissures unite in immense caverns. After the lead was extracted, the miners turned to zinc, or "dry bone" (the name comes from its appearance resembling dried bone material).

Dr. Stephen Langworthy moved with his family to Dubuque in 1834 to join his elder sons. He worked as a government land agent during the Franklin Pierce administration, as well as at his medical practice. He claimed 160 acres with Solon in the Couler Valley area. In 1837, he built a home in Section Eleven of what is today Dubuque Township. Solon hauled rails from the timber with his four yoke of oxen and fenced in a 60-acre plot. He ploughed the field where previously native women had raised corn. There exists no description of their first house other than that of a sixteen-by-sixteen-foot dwelling built against a huge rock protruding from the bluff that he used as a foundation for the fireplace. According to the 1840 federal census, nine people lived there. With no plat maps existing during this time, there is no exact location for the house. An old house located within the

The home of Dr. Stephen and Jane Langworthy, Couler Valley, Dubuque. *Iowa Department of Transportation, Ames Office.*

described legal area existed until it was torn down in 1996. The *Dubuque Telegraph Herald* mentions in an article dating June 26, 1867, that the home of Stephen Langworthy had been sold at a public sale to Alfred Cartigney and the Henry Pfotzer Brewery. The Office of the Iowa State Archaeologist conducted a dig at the suspected location of the home. Specimens found indicate a pre–Civil War era house on the site (possibly even the 1840s). A map from 1866 did show a house at the site, so a conclusion could be made that it was the Langworthy home.

Dr. Stephen Langworthy was instrumental in the future founding of the Dubuque Medical Society. Quackery in the name of medicine flooded the frontier in this era. The first Constitutional Assembly considered regulating the medical profession but rejected the proposal, stating, "No legal enactments would affect reform in the practice of physics and restrict the expensive prevalence of quackery." The first hospital in Dubuque was private and located across from the courthouse at Seventh and Clay (Central) Streets. The Catholic Sisters of Mercy opened Mercy Hospital in 1879, while Finley opened its doors in 1890. Before these events, medical treatment depended on doctors traveling the countryside as Dr. Langworthy did—or, sadly, quackery. A newspaper article of 1928 wrote the following about Dr. Stephen Langworthy: "He and other early doctors dared the rigors and dangers of the country newly opened to settlers under great hardships, forgetting their own comfort and sacrificing in many ways to render a humanitarian service whenever the call to do so came to them."

In 1833, James Langworthy, eldest son of Dr. Stephen Langworthy, helped to build the log Methodist Meeting House in what is today Washington Park. The park occupies a full city block bordered by Sixth and Seventh Streets between Locust and Bluff Streets. The meeting house was used as a schoolhouse and for court. James constructed the second brick home in Dubuque at the corner of Twelfth and Iowa Streets in 1838. The home had a stone fence and a complex of brick stables and outbuildings. It was described as the "finest residence in town." James Langworthy married Agnes Milne of Scotland in 1840. They had six children, with four surviving to adulthood. James served in the state constitutional convention in 1844 and one term in the territorial legislature as a free trade Democrat. The state constitution, drafted in 1844, was rejected by the public due to border disputes to the north, west and south. In 1846, James Langworthy's family sailed to Europe for a six-month tour of various countries. When they returned, they continued to live in the home on Twelfth Street that had been built with bricks from the Langworthy brickyard. In 1850, a new, grander home called Ridgemount on the bluff at the corner of Peabody and James Streets became their new home.

The home on Twelfth and Iowa Streets became home to the Alexander College in 1853. Promoters claimed that this Presbyterian education experiment would become the Yale of Iowa. Joshua Phelps, the pastor of the First Presbyterian Church in Dubuque, served as president of the new college. Just 107 boys enrolled in the preparatory department, while 2 boys began their college studies. The college held classes in German, Latin and Greek, natural science, mathematics, philosophy, astronomy and "less important classes." Funding questions concerning a new building near present-day Finley Hospital led to disagreement and President Phelps's resignation. The college closed in 1859. Alexander Simplot, a famous local artist, began his studies there. In 1874, the remaining walls of the defunct college collapsed; according to the *Telegraph Herald*, it "terrified the neighbors." Nothing remains of Alexander College other than the name College Street, on which its building once stood.

Ridgemount, according to contemporary commentators, was the "finest dwelling north of New Orleans." Made of hand-hewn timbers twelve inches by twelve feet, the house possessed seven chimneys, marble fireplaces and a first floor of smooth-dressed native limestone in its thirty-nine rooms. A captain's watch facing the Mississippi River allowed residents and visitors to scan the river for arriving steamboats. Furnishings for the home bought in New York City arrived in Dubuque via ship to the Gulf of Mexico and steamboats up the Mississippi River. In 1858, Miss Mary Grey, a niece of Mrs. Langworthy's from Scotland, moved into the Langworthy home due to the deaths of her parents. She was only twelve years old and had sailed aboard the *Arabia* across the Atlantic alone. The Langworthys later assumed responsibility for two other homeless cousins. Mary always referred to Ridgemount as "The Pines." The estate included stables, cow sheds and other outbuildings. Mary loved riding the horses stabled there, as horse training and racing was a hobby of the Langworthys. When Colonel Henderson and his soldiers returned from the Civil War in 1863, the Langworthy family sponsored a horse show in their honor.

The home later passed to the Massey family when Fred and Alleen Langworthy Massey returned to Dubuque permanently in 1906. They bought out Augusta Langworthy's interest in the estate and modernized the home. They added electric lights as well as their art treasures. Alleen Langworthy Massey lived there until her death in 1919. The second daughter of James and Agnes Langworthy, Mary Augusta, continued residing at Ridgemount until her death in 1930. After the death of Miss Augusta Langworthy, the contents of the house were sold, including a cup once owned by Frederick the Great of Prussia and the Napoleonic clock that played twelve different tunes. The house then fell into disrepair, but in 1933, the Visiting Nurse Association used it as a fresh air camp for children.

The fresh air camps sponsored by the VNA began in Dubuque in 1911 at the Wartburg Theological Seminary and then moved to Rhomberg Park at the intersection of Shiras and Rhomberg Avenues. This one-square-block area allowed children to live in tents supplied by city residents and receive much-needed medical treatment and nourishment from the VNA for the six-week-long program. In 1933, the camp moved to Ridgemount. The *Telegraph Herald* reported that "once again the happy laughter of children could be heard in the halls of *Ridgemount.*" Sadly, the home no longer exists. In 1945, the expansion of Mercy Hospital resulted in its demolition.

A bit of scandal involving Ridgemount and the Langworthy family occurred in 1904, when Massey Harris, grandson of James and Agnes Langworthy, eloped with Nora O'Halloran, the daughter of John O'Halloran of Dubuque. Nora was a machine operator at the H.B. Glover Company. Massey Harris had lived at Ridgemount with the Masseys since his mother, Clara Langworthy Harris, died suddenly when he was only two years old. Massey and Nora were married in Hammond, Indiana, by a justice of the peace. After the wedding, they returned to Chicago—where his father, Lindley Massey Harris, lived—to beg for forgiveness. After receiving absolution, they lived in Chicago with Mr. Harris.

The H.B. Glover Company held a fascinating place in local history as well. The company employed mostly women who made menswear. The company pioneered adjustable pajamas and the "pocketeer" in overalls to

Ridgemount, the home of James and Agnes Langworthy. *Encyclopedia Dubuque.*

Fresh air camp at the Langworthy home. *Encyclopedia Dubuque.*

hold workers' tools. In 1890, a strike at the company inspired the son of the president, Richard Bissell of Dubuque, to write *7½ Cents*. The book went on to become the hit Broadway play *The Pajama Game* in 1955 and a movie of the same name in 1957 featuring Doris Day and John Riatt. The H.B. Glover Company closed in 1955. The Pendleton Works purchased the machinery and shipped it to its factory in Portland, Oregon.

Edward Langworthy became the wealthiest of the brothers, but his early days were in contrast to his later life. He worked on the family farm in Diamond Grove for five years. They raised wheat, corn and livestock. At first, they also raised cotton. Used for clothing and household goods, the cotton had to be picked, cleaned, spun and woven by family members. This intensive work occurred on the frontier in every household, as goods from the eastern mills were too expensive, if they could even be purchased on the frontier. Once steamships made trade and travel more cost efficient, the home cotton industry ceased, as products could be purchased from the East. Edward noted that since very little money existed on the frontier, barter was the main mode of exchange.

Edward Langworthy. *Center for Dubuque History, Loras College.*

In 1827, he and his brother Lucius and sisters Mary Ann and Maria moved to Galena. His description of the journey follows: "We took a wagon to Quincy [Illinois] and a steamer to the rapids where we stayed at Fort Edwards [Warsaw] opposite Keokuk [Iowa]. We procured a pirogue and spent ten days going to Rock Island rowing, poling, cordeling and bushwhacking along in the boiling sun of June." In the confusion of disembarking from the steamboat, they left behind a part of their luggage containing buckskin clothing intended for use when mining. At Rock Island, Illinois, they boarded a keelboat with an experienced crew. Edward described this journey as a "delightful trip": "We walked the water like a thing of life and the merry song of the boatmen enlivened the scene." They arrived at Galena, which he described as "not being on the Mississippi River but on the Fever River and called Houghton's Bay." From Galena they traveled to Buncombe, where James had a store. Edward bought a small claim near Council Hill that earned him $100 per month. He built a cabin there. He said of his cabin, "In the morning we used to get out of our wet bed, build a fire out of wet wood and cook breakfast and go to work." One wonders if he could imagine the extravagant home of his future.

Edward began mining with his brothers. Lead sold for five dollars per one thousand pounds so most miners were poor and many were destitute. Famine stalked every settlement. As a result, many miners left for Missouri or Illinois. Edward wrote of these difficult days, "I have but few pleasing memories of these years and shall, therefore, pass over them as briefly as possible." The Langworthys, who had done better than most small claim holders, divided their supplies among the needy and left for Galena. Edward returned in 1831 with hogs. They flourished in the countryside and provided much-needed food for the miners. In 1832, Edward was farming and mining near Platteville, Wisconsin, until the Black Hawk War interrupted. Miners usually came to an area to make a fortune and then left. They did not believe that corn, wheat or other grains could be grown in "this cold country." They also did not want to use valuable time farming when they needed to mine for lead. Edward Langworthy noted, "[A]t first small gardens—potatoes and cabbage were planted. Then a bold miner determined to try the experiment and actually planted some corn in his garden. It proved a success." Farming rapidly came to surpass mining as an occupation on the frontier.

Edward Langworthy served three terms in the territorial legislature. He was also a trustee of Dubuque and a city alderman. The Legislative Assembly met in Burlington, Iowa, on November 4, 1839. Stephen Hempstead of Dubuque was the council president, while Edward Langworthy represented Dubuque in the House of Representatives. The assembly adjourned on January 17, 1840, with an extra session held on July 13, 1840. In 1844, Edward was a member of the state constitutional convention, which met in Iowa City from October 7 to November 1. Fifty-three Democrats and seventeen Whigs constructed a state constitution for Iowa, but it was voted down by the citizens of the state on August 4, 1848, due to a dispute over boundaries. Edward had voted to exclude African Americans and abolish the grand jury system, but neither measure passed. The Second Constitutional Convention convened in Iowa City on May 4, 1846, but Thomas McCraney represented Dubuque, not Edward Langworthy. This constitution was successfully adopted, and Iowa became a state in 1846. Iowa's constitution is one of the oldest state constitutions still in effect.

Of his early days at the Dubuque lead mines, Edward remarked that "nowhere had there ever been such honesty, integrity and high toned generosity as was found among the miners in the early days." Since the Langworthys were diversifying their interests, moving closer to town became

Edward Langworthy's gold watch.
Brad Chalmers.

necessary. Edward built his first home in Greek Revival style at Fourteenth and White Streets in 1838, complete with orchards and a large garden. James joined him in the area, as did Solon. Other businessmen soon followed. Judge Dyer built a stately home (with columns similar to those at Mount Vernon) at Main and Thirteenth Street. When George Wallace Jones abandoned the downtown district and built his mansion on Julien Avenue (University Street), it signaled the beginning of the move to the bluffs overlooking the city and river, away from the business district. The times were changing, and the people with them.

ROUGH AND TOUGH LIFE
ON A MINING FRONTIER

etsey Woodbury Massey had married Stephen Langworthy on November 4, 1777, and gave birth to twelve Langworthy children before her death in 1820 along with her young son, Stephen, of malaria. Betsey's brother Dr. Isaiah Massey had moved his family to Illinois along with the Langworthys. When he died of malaria after his trip to Diamond Grove with nephew James Langworthy, his children—Woodbury, Benjamin, Henry L. and Louisa—remained with their Langworthy cousins. They later accompanied the Langworthys to Galena and Dubuque. Henry Massey, who had served under General Dodge in the Black Hawk War, opened a harness shop in Galena. Woodbury along with his wife, Maria, and child moved to Dubuque. Benjamin and Louisa arrived in Dubuque with the other Langworthy daughters.

Since Dubuque was officially part of Michigan Territory and in 1836 became part of Wisconsin Territory, the closest justice system was hundreds of miles away in Detroit and then Green Bay. As a result of this distance, law and order on the mining frontier had to be a local affair out of necessity. The case of Patrick O'Connor demonstrated this point clearly. O'Connor, born in Ireland in 1797, came to Galena, Illinois, to mine lead in 1826. Two years later, he suffered a broken leg, which had to be amputated. His fellow miners willingly paid for his medical and living expenses. O'Connor's behavior soon lost him both the charity and support of the community. He burned down his cabin in an effort to secure more funds and nearly destroyed surrounding property. When a Galena merchant, Mr. Brophy, exposed

O'Connor's criminal behavior, O'Connor burst into his store and fired off his gun in an attempt to kill Brophy. Now facing the charge of attempted murder, O'Connor left Galena for Dubuque. In Dubuque, he partnered with George O'Keaf. They built a cabin south of Dubuque and began a mining operation. On May 9, 1834, Mr. O'Keaf and a friend returned to the cabin with provisions but found the door locked. O'Connor refused to open the door, so O'Keaf forced it open only to be shot and killed by O'Connor. The friend escaped by running to the smelting furnace of Wilson and Hulett. An assembly of miners returned to the cabin, where O'Connor waited. His only reply to the question of why he shot his partner was that it was his business.

The first thought of his fellow miners was to hang him immediately, but cooler heads prevailed, and he was taken into Dubuque, where on May 29, 1834, the first trial for murder in Dubuque was held under a large elm tree. Captain White was appointed the prosecuting attorney, and Captain Bates from Galena was the defense attorney. Members of the jury included Woodbury Massey, Hosea T. Camp, James McKenzie, Milo Prentice, Jesse Harrison, Thomas McCraney, Antoine Loire and Nicholas Carroll. O'Connor believed that since no law existed in the territory, they had no right to put him on trial. Captain Bates wanted O'Connor sent to Galena, where he could be tried by a legal court, but since others who had been sent there had been freed due to Illinois having no jurisdiction at the Dubuque mines, it was decided to continue the trial at the present location. Witnesses were heard, and after an hour of deliberations, a guilty verdict with a death sentence by hanging was announced. Applications to the governor of Missouri and the president of the United States to pardon him were denied, as they replied that they had no jurisdiction.

Rumors that miners from Mineral Point, Wisconsin, were coming to rescue O'Connor roused the miners to action. Under the command of Loring Wheeler as their elected captain, 163 men lined Main Street. They then elected W.I. Madden, Woodbury Massey, Thomas Brasher, John Smith and Milo Prentice as "Marshalls of the Day." Marching to the accompaniment of a fife playing the death march as spectators gathered, stores closed and passengers from two steamboats from Galena (including the *Jo Daviess*, piloted by Daniel Harris) and Prairie du Chien disembarked to witness the hanging, they arrived at the house of Herman Chadwick, where O'Connor was held. O'Connor rode on his own casket in a wagon to the gallows at the present site of the courthouse. No one arrived to rescue O'Connor. He was hanged at noon after admitting that he murdered O'Keaf and begging forgiveness. The first capital punishment in what became the state of Iowa was now history.

With government officials a distant help, local residents usually handled crime themselves. When a man named Leek stole a canoe owned by Thomas McCraney and loaded it with lead already stacked by the owners near the river for shipment, he was followed all the way to Rock Island. Apprehended there, he was brought back to the Dubuque Mines, where he received thirty-nine lashes of a whip and was exiled across the Mississippi River. A known wife beater was tarred and feathered before he was sent packing across the river.

When an enslaved man, Ralph, who was brought to the lead mines by his owner and then forced to return south, was rescued by a group of Dubuque miners in Rock Island, Judge Wilson (Dubuque) of the Territorial Supreme Court heard his case and found that he was indeed free, as slavery was illegal in the territory. In his comments on this case, Lucius Langworthy praised Ralph's rescuers as "liberty loving citizens who did not allow the fear of being called abolitionists" to deter them. Unfortunately, a year later, he did not adhere to these same sentiments when Nathaniel Morgan, a free Black man and resident of Dubuque who was a member of the Methodist Church, was beaten to death by a mob because they thought he had stolen a trunk of clothes. Mr. Langworthy maintained that the mob acted with "mistaken zeal and with entire ignorance perhaps of the injury they were inflicting. No doubt the men who inflicted this wrong regretted their rashness and folly too late." There was no evidence of the theft by Nathaniel Morgan or of any regret on the part of the mob.

Not all time was spent working or fighting. Reverend Bastain preached in the log Methodist church. Mrs. Whitmore taught classes during the week in the same log building, in what is now Washington Square. Balls and parties were common. Poker, euchre and brag were the favorite card games. Older than poker, brag was a British gambling game; it was traditionally played with three cards but also could be played with five, seven or nine cards. In brag, each player must bet or leave the game—there is no passing. Players must match or raise the bet until only two players remain. At that point, either one player leaves or "stacks" the game, allowing the other player to win without showing his cards. Alternatively, a player can bet twice the amount, thus forcing a showdown. The player with the highest-ranking hand wins.

On July 4, 1836, an Independence Day celebration occurred in Dubuque with Father Mazzuchelli officiating as chaplain. Milo Prentice read the Declaration of Independence, and Dr. Stephen Langworthy reigned as president of the day. Music, speeches, patriotism and dancing filled the day. In the evening, a public dinner honored Governor Henry Dodge. Lucius

Langworthy said in a speech that "we all came together and refreshed our recollections returning heartfelt gratitude to God for the blessings which His kind providence had permitted this nation to enjoy."

Sensational events on a mining frontier happened with frequency. One occurred in 1835 that involved several prominent community members. Woodbury Massey, his brothers and sister were among the first of Dubuque settlers when they arrived with their Langworthy cousins. Woodbury donated $225 for the construction (the largest single donation) of the Methodist church, erected in the city, as well as was involved in many other community endeavors. He married Maria Coonce from Missouri. Her father, Nicholas Coonce, was well known in St. Charles County, Missouri. He had been captured by the Kickapoo, who held him prisoner for two years. He attempted to escape, but his captors apprehended him, scalped him and left him for dead. Very much alive, he immigrated to Missouri in 1790. Nicholas served in the War of 1812, escorted William Clark to Fort Sage and owned 956 arpens (approximately 1,100 acres) of land. It was said of him that he hunted a great deal, was afraid of nothing and crawled into hollow trees and dens where bears were sleeping to feel if they were fat enough to kill. Nicholas Coonce died in 1820 after falling from a horse.

Woodbury and Maria Massey had two sons, Henry and Solon Lycurgas, and two daughters, Maria and Sarah. Mr. Massey had purchased a lot and mineral lode with a disputed claim. The Smiths, William and son, held that they, not Massey, owned both the land and mineral lode. A legal suit decided against the Smiths, but they were not to be deterred. Hiding on the claim, they shot Massey through the heart when he arrived. The Smiths were apprehended, charged with murder and held until the session of the circuit court met at Mineral Point, Wisconsin. The defense objected as the jurisdiction of the circuit court was questionable. The court agreed and freed the Smiths. After their release, the defendants vacated the region temporarily.

The younger brother of Woodbury Massey promised to kill the assassins if he ever saw them. The opportunity came soon. Henry Massey observed the elder Smith strolling down the streets of Galena. He quickly fetched his pistol and killed him. He was never arrested or tried. In fact, citizens viewed the death of the elder Smith as necessary.

The younger Smith, however, did not agree with this opinion. Upon returning to the mines, he vowed to kill one or both of the remaining Massey brothers. Louisa Massey, age sixteen, feared for her brothers. She disguised herself and sought out Smith. She found him on Main Street, demanded that he defend himself and shot him in the chest. Louisa fled to a friendly house, then to her brother's home and finally, in the morning, to Galena. Smith was very lucky that day. In his chest pocket he had carried a wallet filled with papers. These papers slowed the bullet so he revived, determined to seek out Louisa Massey; he died several years later from the wound. The townspeople, outraged over the ongoing violence, called a miners' meeting to address the jurisdiction problems. They threatened to use the services of "Judge Lynch" if the criminals did not leave the city within thirty-six hours. Many, including the younger Smith, took the advice and fled.

Louisa's return to Dubuque from Galena was greeted with such enthusiasm that the steamboat carrying her almost sank as greeters attempted to meet her. She later married Mr. S.J. Williamson. To honor her role in the founding of the state, Louisa County in southeast Iowa is only one of two counties in Iowa with female names. The second is Pocahontas in north-central Iowa. Maria Massey, widow of Woodbury Massey, returned to Missouri. She later married Benjamin Massey, brother of Woodbury, Henry and Louisa. They had three children: William Coonce, Nicholas and Silas.

An odd robbery took place in September 1879 at the office of Solon Langworthy. While he was out of the office and the door locked, a passing teamster heard a window being forced open. He investigated and found two men jumping out of the window and running toward White Street. When he tried to stop them, one of the men threatened him with a large knife. Further inspection revealed that nothing had been taken, although several pages of a ledger under the letter *L* had been torn out and stolen. In 1891, upon the eighty-third birthday of Edward Langworthy, he received a check for $23.50 from a woman in Bismarck, North Dakota. Apparently, she had owed him money from forty-seven years earlier for the sale of a bull and believed it time to repay her debt; different responses to the Langworthy businesses, but responses nonetheless.

HOW DO WE GET THERE FROM HERE?

Both Dubuque, Iowa, and the Langworthy family increased in number and prospered. All owed much of this growth to the Mississippi River. It served as the major artery of commerce and travel. The canoes, keelboats and pirogues of the past soon made way for the steamboats. This new mode of transportation brought speed, efficiency, profit, romance and even luxury to the world of travel. The number of steamboats to dock at Dubuque rapidly increased from 231 in 1834 to 672 in 1843. Steamboating was not without danger, and as with most new technologies, its days were numbered.

Daniel Smith Harris and Sarah Marie Langworthy, daughter of Stephen and Betsey Langworthy, married in May 1833. Harris entered into the steamboat traffic business between Galena and St. Louis with his brother Scribe Harris. The Harris brothers and their father, whose ancestry reached back to the *Mayflower*, had arrived in Galena with Dr. Moses Meeker in 1823. The trip on the keelboat *Colonel Bumford* from Cincinnati took thirty-one days using poles and sails. While they labored up the river, the first machine-driven boat on the upper Mississippi, *Virginia*, passed them. Daniel Harris never forgot that sight. His father began farming and planted the first orchard in Galena. Their mother and three brothers joined them in 1824. Daniel and Scribe prospected for lead when time permitted. They struck lead at the West Diggings but had to mine part time, as their father mandated that they attend school. A claim jumper attempted to steal their mine, since he insisted no law existed in the region. When the would-be thief arrived to work the mine, he found the brothers armed and ready to defend their claim.

He fled and never returned. West Diggings yielded 4 million pounds of lead and the profits for their next endeavor. In 1829, at the age of twenty-one, Daniel Smith Harris began his career on the river by signing on as a cub pilot to Captain David Bates on the *Galena*. Scribe signed on as an engineer. Fate stepped in to stop their plans when, in October, their father died of cholera. The brothers returned to the farm to support their mother and younger brothers. Again fate intervened when in 1832 Daniel served as a captain in the army during the Black Hawk War, moving him off the farm.

Captain Daniel Harris. *National Mississippi River Museum and Aquarium.*

Once out of the army, Daniel and Scribe Harris, who married Phoebe Reeder, the sister of Paulina and Mary Francis Langworthy, launched their steamboat business. (In an interesting note, the Reeder family was related to the Wright brothers of flight history.) They built the steamboat *Jo Daviess* themselves from what was described by observers as junk that Scribe had purchased in Cincinnati. The *Jo Daviess* was ninety feet long, with a fifteen-foot-wide beam. On the way to St. Louis, another steamboat attempted to pass. Unwilling to lose, Daniel carried his rifle to the pilothouse and shot through the pilothouse of the opposing boat as it drew alongside. This event helped to establish his reputation as a man with a red-hot temper, purple language and ironclad honesty. They soon added the *Smelter* to their fleet, built during 1836–37. With this new boat, they could make the trip from Cincinnati to Galena in twenty-one days. In one very fast run, Daniel made the same trip in five days. As their business prospered, they added more steamboats. Their fame was such that each trip was fully booked. Captain Harris won nearly every race he entered and never had a boiler explode—a common disaster on steamboats. Captain Harris was so proud of the *Smelter* that he even mounted a cannon on board to announce their arrival in port. As the territory west of the Mississippi opened, they carried passengers intending to settle the new lands. His determination to be the first to break through the ice in the spring allowed him to win free harbor, docking seven times between the years 1844 and 1861—a feat unequaled.

The Langworthy brothers and Orrin Smith, their brother-in-law, decided that if Harris "can be so successful on a shoestring, why can't we be much more fortunate with our capital." In 1835, they invested in steamboats. Captain Harris, however, was determined to beat them at every chance. Thus began a fifteen-year feud between them. One can only imagine the conversations around the table at Langworthy family dinners and celebrations.

As both sides accumulated more capital and new boats, the feud became increasingly bitter. In 1848, Smith and the Langworthy brothers organized the Minnesota Packet Company, whose most important boat was the *Dr. Franklin*, the fastest steamboat on the Mississippi River. Harris countered with the *Senator*, a boat he acknowledged was "but little slower." Competition between the two companies was so intense that the cost of a passenger trip from Galena to St. Paul sank to fifty cents, while a barrel of flour cost only ten cents to ship the same distance. Captain Harris decided to sell the *Senator* to the Minnesota Packet Company and retire. Again fate intervened when Congress opened the Minnesota Territory to settlement. Harris could not resist. Back to the river he went, with even faster boats. By 1850, the competition between the family members had become unbearable. In the spring, the Harris brothers came up the river with the *West Newton*, so the Langworthys and Smith built an even faster boat, the *Nominee*. By the fall of 1850, everyone desired a compromise. They decided to merge into a new edition of the Minnesota Packet Company, with Captain Smith as president and Captain Harris as a director. They pooled their boats and earnings.

Captain Smith—already a wealthy man from his mining, smelting, steamboating and partnership in the wholesale grocery firm of Smith and Campbell in Galena—became the mayor of Galena in 1844. His mansion still stands on Park Avenue in Galena, Illinois. The merger, however, did not end the rivalry concerning just who had the fastest boat on the Mississippi River. In 1852, Captain Smith raced his boat, *Nominee*, against the *West Newton*, belonging to Captain Harris, from Galena to St. Paul. At a record speed of twelve and a half miles per hour, Captain Smith won. Unfortunately, the *Nominee* sank at Britt's Landing in 1854, located in Vernon County, Wisconsin, halfway between Stoddard and Genoa.

The Grand Excursion of 1854 caused thousands of people to board the trains in Chicago and travel to Rock Island, Illinois, to celebrate the first railroad to reach the Mississippi River. The celebration then moved to the river when 1,200 people boarded steamboats for a tour of the Upper Mississippi. Former president Millard Fillmore joined the excursion, led by Captain Harris on board the *War Eagle*, which included stops at Galena and Dubuque. Little did Captain Harris realize, as he began the

The home of Captain Orrin and Mary Ann Langworthy Smith, Galena, Illinois. *Photo by author.*

upriver journey past the construction of a bridge, that he was witnessing the end of the steamboat and his career. The new bridge carried the railroad west of the Mississippi River and redirected commerce east and west rather than north and south along the river. Chicago, as a result, became the focus of rail transportation. With the Civil War looming on the horizon, the switch to east–west trade and travel rather than north–south accentuated economic benefits for the Midwest as well. When the South cut itself off from the North by seceding from the Union in 1861, the

The home of Captain Daniel and Sarah Langworthy Harris, Galena, Illinois. *Randy von Liski Photography, flickr.com/photos/myoldpostcards.*

economies of the Midwest were less affected than those of the South due to the railroad networks.

While sitting on the porch of his Galena home, Captain Harris whittled his own design for a new steamboat. Built in 1857, the side-wheeler *Grey Eagle* was long, narrow and fast at 295 feet in length with a 55-foot-wide beam. It was so fast, in fact, that other boats refused to race it. In 1858, *Grey Eagle* reached St. Paul first with the news that the Atlantic cable had been laid to connect New York and London. *Grey Eagle*'s speed topped thirteen miles per hour against a four-to-five-mile-per-hour current. Captain Harris radiated pride as he piloted the undisputed fastest boat on the Mississippi River.

Meanwhile, the new Rock Island Railroad Bridge reached completion. The steamboat companies sued the railroad for blocking navigation at an already difficult section of the river due to the rapids at Rock Island. Abraham Lincoln was the lawyer for the Rock Island Railroad. The steamboat companies lost the lawsuit. The rapids were called the "gate of death," and the addition of the bridge complicated navigation so much that the riverboat captains referred to it as the invention of "Satan and the Rock Island Railroad." In May 1861, Captain Harris, who always took the wheel at the rapids, steered *Grey Eagle* and its fifty-eight passengers into the treacherous stretch of river. With a sickening *crunch*, the boat hit the stone abutment of the bridge, tearing away the wheelhouse and most of the deck. The shock of the crash threw the boat against the Iowa pier and crushed its hull. The fifty-foot-high smokestacks fell into the water. The *Grey Eagle* sank in twenty feet of river. Six people died, including Mrs. Weaver and her four-year-old son from Dyersville, Iowa. Captain Harris's boat, worth $60,000, lay crushed at the bottom of the Mississippi River. He was able to salvage the 320-pound carved eagle that had adorned his boat. It is now located at the Putnam Museum and Science Center in Davenport, Iowa, despite the many protests of Galena residents.

Captain Harris retired to his home and family in Galena. His first wife, Sarah Marie Langworthy—sister of James, Solon, Edward and Lucius—died in Cuba on January 25, 1850. She had gone to Cuba for her health, as she suffered from consumption (or tuberculosis). Caused by bacteria, tuberculosis by 1800 had killed one in seven people who had ever lived. In 1882, Robert Koch discovered the bacteria that caused this disease, thus ruling out the suspected hereditary causes for this dreaded affliction. Sanatoriums were established to isolate infected individuals but also to offer better nutrition, improved climate and rest. It was not until the twentieth century and the advent of antibiotics that tuberculosis was able to be controlled.

Daniel and Sarah Langworthy Harris had five children. Her death left him with a young family of ages two years to fifteen years. In 1851, he married Sarah Coates, who entered medical school at the age of forty-five. She graduated as one of the first women doctors in the United States and practiced medicine in Galena. In 1869, she presided over the Grand Women Suffrage Convention in Galena. Both Elizabeth Cady Stanton and Susan B. Anthony attended the convention. Daniel and Sarah Coates had seven children, five of whom reached adulthood.

In 1879, Daniel Harris visited President Grant. Grant had given Harris a cigar when Grant was a general in the Union army during the Civil War, but Harris vowed not to smoke it until Grant became president. When elected president of the United States, Grant awarded him another cigar, but Harris vowed not to smoke it until Grant was elected to a second term. So, when he visited Grant again in 1879, he, of course, requested and received another cigar. Captain Harris died on March 17, 1893, in his eighty-fifth year. Their Gothic Revival home on Prospect Street in Galena is the Steamboat House B&B. According to local lore, it was a station on the Underground Railroad, complete with a tunnel. Captain Harris was named a member of the National Rivers Hall of Fame in 1993.

Daniel Smith Harris Jr., born in Galena in 1843 to Daniel Harris and Sarah Marie Langworthy, married Kathleen Ott in 1874 in Eureka County,

Carved wooden eagle from Harris's steamboat, *Grey Eagle*. *Putnam Museum, Davenport, Iowa.*

Nevada. While in Nevada, he worked in the famous Comstock silver mine in Virginia City. Searching for greener pastures and his fortune, they moved to San Francisco in 1875. He and Kathleen had a daughter, Alice May, in 1886. They divorced, and Daniel moved to Ketchikan, Alaska, to join the thousands infected with gold fever from 1897 to 1906. In 1900, Ketchikan was incorporated with four hundred residents. It rapidly became the mining supply center, with six saloons, one church, four restaurants, four doctors, two assay offices, one U.S. marshal, two hotels and much more. Daniel arrived in Alaska with John Schoenbar, who had been a business associate in the gold and silver business in Eureka, Nevada. Apparently, Schoenbar was a con man who left Harris destitute and died himself on the streets of Oakland California. Harris went on to work in Ketchikan. He organized the fire department and devoted his efforts to public service. Ketchikan named a street in his honor as a tribute to his service. Daniel Smith Harris died in Sitka, Alaska, on April 26, 1926.

In June 1946, Daniel Robert Drake, the infant great-great-grandson of Captain Daniel Harris and Sarah Langworthy Harris, and his parents boarded the first boat to reestablish passenger travel on the Upper Mississippi River. Accompanying them was Captain Mary B. Greene, the only licensed woman pilot and captain on the Mississippi River. As a tribute to his family history and the history of steamboating on the Mississippi River, young Daniel was baptized on board the boat, with his godmother, Captain Mary B. Greene, witnessing.

Captain Orrin Smith and Mary Ann Langworthy Smith had ten children. Their Greek Revival home is located on Park Avenue in Galena, Illinois, across the street from Grant Park. Captain Orrin Smith was known as a very religious man, so his steamboats never left dock on a Sunday. He was one of the founders of Winona, Minnesota, as well. After the end of his steamboating career, they lived in Chicago from 1866 to 1871. There in 1871, his home and brick business were destroyed in the Great Chicago Fire. Mary Ann Langworthy Smith died on June 12, 1881, and Captain Smith followed on October 30, 1881. They are buried at Linwood Cemetery in Dubuque, Iowa, to be close to kinsmen and friends.

River travel eased transportation difficulties, but not all of them. To bring produce to city markets and to take supplies back to the farms, roads had to be built. Road construction on the Iowa frontier faced many obstacles, including the many streams and rivers that needed to be crossed. Wetlands bogged down wagons; mud in the spring and ice in the winter stopped travelers. Floods, snow—the list continued. The people on the frontier had tackled other challenges, so they saw the road issue as just another one.

Near Key West, Iowa, now part of Dubuque, there is a bronze plaque that reads, "This Highway is the Old Military Road constructed originally in 1839 by James L. and Lucius H. Langworthy as a portion of the Government road extending from Dubuque to the Northern Boundary of Missouri." Modern travelers drive past the sign and toward Iowa City or Cedar Rapids without notice. Have you ever wondered why the villages of Langworthy south of Monticello or Solon just north of Iowa City have the names of a founding family of Dubuque?

After the Black Hawk Purchase of 1833, Dubuque became the port of entry into the new territory due to its proximity to the established settlement in Galena. Supplies for the journey west were purchased here, but to travel in those days was, as one traveler stated, "a torment."

While the Mississippi River opened the area to outside exploration, travel inland meant mud, swamps, floods, trees, snow and ice—impossible obstacles for settlement. The answer was simple: build roads. The solution, however, was not simple. Money, as always, was the problem. In 1826, a resolution was presented in Congress to fund a road from Dubuque to Missouri, but it was defeated. Federal money for roads within states or territories was a hot political issue. When President Van Buren signed the bill to fund that road in 1839, it had to be defined as a military road for the use of troops and the U.S. mail. Congress authorized $20,000 for the survey of the road.

Settlers were anxious to move into the western regions of the Black Hawk Purchase. Early roads were little more than muddy trails, with no bridges over the many streams and creeks, so improved transportation was essential. To encourage Congress to appropriate money for such a project, the word *military* was added to the bill approving construction of the road, although most of the traffic was civilian. R.C. Tilghman, an engineer and surveyor from Baltimore, hired Lyman Dillon from Cascade, Iowa, to plow a furrow along the approximately one hundred miles from Iowa City to Dubuque. While his achievement has much myth attached to it, we know that he bought five yoke of oxen from Eli Meyers of Iowa City. He hired George and Adam Rohret to assist him. Adam drove the oxen and helped to hold the plow to give Dillon a rest. George drove the wagon with the supplies for Dillon.

The Rohret brothers lived in Johnson County, Iowa. An affidavit sworn before notary Eugene Kean on September 11, 1939, validated the presence of the Rohret brothers. An interesting story about George came to light during research on the plowing of the furrow. Settlers had to pay their personal property taxes in Dubuque. No property taxes on land existed because settlers had no clear title to the preempted land. The Supreme Court decision in the case of *Chouteau v. Molony* settled the title dispute in March 1854, when the court declared the Chouteau claim to Dubuque lands invalid. George and Wenzel Hummer volunteered to carry both their taxes and those of their neighbors to the tax office in Dubuque. One can only imagine the danger of four or five days walking through the wilderness with a sack of money. The coinage used was Mexican or Spanish silver and gold coins, so the bag also became quite heavy. After a successful journey, they returned home. The finished road made this trip much quicker and less dangerous.

Lyman Dillon and his brother were orphaned at an early age, so they lived in an orphanage. Lyman was "put out" to work for a tavern owner. His work was hard and the hours long, leaving no time for schooling or books, so he ran away. He educated himself and eventually attended college in Utica, New York, where he had been born in 1800. With the promise of excellent farmland and potential waterpower, he moved to Cascade, Iowa.

He claimed land two miles north of the village on the north fork of the Maquoketa River, where he operated a sawmill. He was thirty-nine years old when he plowed the now famous furrow. He died in 1867 and is buried in Cascade.

Edward Langworthy wrote, "My brothers James, and Lucius had contracts to make the road from Dubuque to the Cedar River and there was a furrow on one side the whole length of the road." Federal troops rarely used the road, but land seekers did. The road started at Tim Fanning's log tavern in Dubuque, stayed to the high ground, passed through as many county seats as possible and ended at the Lean-back Hall, a temporary tavern at Iowa City. James and Edward Langworthy of Dubuque were contracted to build the road from Dubuque to the Cedar River following the furrow that Lyman Dillon broke with his teams of oxen and a sod-breaking plow. Dillon received three dollars per mile, used ten oxen and had his provisions in a covered wagon driven by George Rohret following the furrow. Today, the route is covered by Highway 151 from Dubuque to Anamosa and Highway 1 to Iowa City. Originally, the Military Road followed State Road 261 as well, but it was decommissioned and replaced by Highway 1. Subsequent grading and changing the course of the highways to eliminate curves has altered the route significantly.

Trees were cut for a forty-foot-wide path and stumps removed from twenty feet of that width. Prairie Creek, Whitewater Creek and Wapsipinicon River had to be bridged. Flooding, a constant problem, had washed out most of the bridges by 1844. The government funded $8,000 to relocate portions of the road and build new bridges. The Western Stage Company offered four horse coaches for safe, speedy (three and a half miles per hour) and comfortable travel to all points between Dubuque and Iowa City. A traveler could leave Dubuque at 3:00 a.m., 4:00 a.m., 8:00 a.m. or 9:00 a.m. from the Stage Office at Second and Main Streets.

Settlements located along the course of the road prospered. The Twelve Mile House was the first stage stop south of Dubuque. While it now exists only in memory, the Twelve Mile House was built by Lemuel Laytton in 1842 and once housed and fed travelers along the Military Road. It started as a log cabin but soon needed more room so a new two-story white frame house replaced the cabin. The house—with green shutters, sleeping rooms, a piano and velvet carpeting in the family living room—impressed visitors. The grounds included a large vegetable garden, flower gardens and an orchard. To those journeying on the road, the stop at the Twelve Mile House was a very welcome respite.

Flour from the mills along the cascade of the North Fork of the Maquoketa River provided "superior" flour for travelers and businesses. Bowen's Prairie, Monticello, Langworthy, Anamosa, Fairview, Martelle, Mount Vernon, Solon and Iowa City were established along the road. Towns not located along the road withered and disappeared. Small communities passed into history once automobile travel allowed residents to easily access larger towns.

Hugh Bowen established Bowen's Prairie after moving there from the Durango lead mines. A schoolhouse, church and post office, along with many dwellings, once occupied the site. Today, the cemetery, with "Bowen's Prairie" across the gate, is the only evidence of a once thriving community. Ivanhoe was located along the Cedar River near Iowa City. Anson Cowles laid out the town and planned a great university, but death ended his elaborate plans. Ivanhoe never grew, but locals knew it to be a haven for horse thieves and counterfeiters.

By 1850, the population of Iowa had swelled to more than 200,000, and during 1851 and 1852, eight hundred wagon teams moved along the road to the gold fields of California—testimony to the value of this road. On May 13, 1927, the Dubuque Chapter of the Daughters of the American Revolution unveiled the marker on the Old Military Road in honor of James and Lucius Langworthy between Key West and Ballyclough. (The tiny settlement of Ballyclough, located at the intersection of Military Road and Swiss Valley Road, was established in 1843 with a post office. First known as Ballyclough Grove, the name was changed to Ballyclough in 1857. The post office closed in 1900.) Henry G. Langworthy unveiled the marker, designed by Susan Valeria Altman, who was the great-great-granddaughter of Lucius Langworthy. Massey Harris (grandson of James Langworthy) assisted Mr. Langworthy at the unveiling. County Supervisor C.W. Datisman delivered a speech, after which the crowd was entertained by the Dubuque High School Band.

It is difficult now to imagine what it must have been like to see Lyman Dillon and the Rohret brothers with the five yoke of oxen plowing a furrow through shoulder-high prairie grass toward the future. Years later, in 1920, two enterprising Iowans retraced the route of Dillon and the Old Military Road. Marcus Hansen and John E. Briggs started from the steps of the Old Capital in Iowa City on a journey to Dubuque. They remarked that many people had no knowledge of the old road, but they were entertained by those few who had memories. They passed through the once prosperous but now extinct village of Ivanhoe and the small town of Langworthy, located south of Monticello and named for the Langworthy brothers of Dubuque. After four days of walking, they finally reached the Julien Hotel in Dubuque with sore feet but a happy sense of accomplishment.

While the Mississippi River offered excellent travel, it had its limitations. Ice in the winter, flooding in the spring, low water in the summer and the constant danger of rapids and snags caused more than a few restrictions. Road construction met even more difficulties. Due to the political issues surrounding the construction of roads within states or regions, federal funds did not exist. Constructing a road through the wilderness proved to be expensive and sometimes impossible. Iowa is blessed with many rivers and wetlands, but crossing them with roads exposed just how expensive and grueling these projects would be.

Ferries offered their services across rivers and streams. In 1833, nineteen licenses for ferries were issued, ten of them for Iowa and five of them in Dubuque. Some area towns still bear the names of these entrepreneurs— Harper's Ferry and Specht's Ferry, Iowa, for example. The ferries caused bottlenecks in travel time and raised the cost. Plank roads laid across swamps and wetlands protected the traveler from being bogged in mud but were very expensive. Maintenance of these primitive roads, if it could be called maintenance, was sporadic at best. A solution to the transportation woes of the frontier soon appeared on the eastern horizon, and the Langworthy family played a major role once again.

Lucius Langworthy worked with John Plumbe Jr. and Asa Whitney to build a Pacific railroad to the West Coast. John Plumbe was a man ahead of his time. Born in Wales in 1809, he arrived in Dubuque in 1836 as a land speculator. Both he and the Langworthys understood the importance of a railroad connection to the markets of the East and for settlement of the West. Unfortunately, their vision was not appreciated or understood.

In 1836, the Belmont and Dubuque Railroad incorporated and formed the Louisiana Company. Investors paid $15,000 to buy eighty acres in Wisconsin along the Mississippi River. Lots were platted and sold for a new town of Sinipee, named for a hollow there. Sinipee (also Sinnipee) was to be the jumping-off point for the transcontinental railroad to connect with the Oregon Territory. Congress did appropriate $2,000 for a survey route to Sinipee. On November 10, 1838, the government established a post office in Sinipee, with Plumbe as postmaster. A brickyard, tinsmith, shoe shop, blacksmith, cabinet shop and homes soon followed. Steamboats docked there. George Wallace Jones, who was a delegate from the Wisconsin Territory, presented a resolution to Congress for the appropriation of funds to carry out Plumbe's plan. The proposal contained the establishment of a joint stock company, with one share worth ten dollars, offered to everyone in the United States. The railroad was to be managed by a board of directors, with one director from each state or territory. The money would have covered the cost of the first division of the line, with public lands to be granted to the railroad for the cost of construction. Members of Congress laughed. They said they might as well try to build a railroad to the moon.

In 1855, Secretary of War Jefferson Davis (a close friend of George Wallace Jones) published a survey for a transcontinental railroad following Plumbe's route. He gave no credit to Plumbe. John Plumbe Jr. committed suicide on May 30, 1857.

In December 1844, another public meeting, held for the purpose of constructing a railroad to connect Dubuque to Lake Michigan, authorized Edward Langworthy, Timothy Davis, L.A. Thomas and General James Wilson to travel to Madison to secure the cooperation of the territorial legislature in a petition to Congress for a railroad. They successfully obtained a charter for a railroad in place of the Belmont and Dubuque Railroad that had not been built. This, too, came to nothing.

Asa Whitney proposed a transcontinental railroad to Congress in 1845 but met with derision and opposition as well. Finally, in 1861, President Lincoln signed the Pacific Railroad Act, which led to the completion of the Transcontinental Railroad in 1869. By this late date, neither Sinipee nor Dubuque were included in the route.

Railroads did come eventually to Dubuque. In 1848, Caleb Booth, former mayor of Dubuque, held a meeting in Dubuque of prominent citizens in which they passed a resolution favoring a railroad to be built from Lake Michigan to Jordan's Ferry opposite Dubuque. Lucius Langworthy was selected to write to Congress concerning this resolution. In May 1848, a railroad convention convened in Dubuque. Resolutions from this convention favored the construction of railroads and the sale of stock to do so. Peter Lorimier and Lucius Langworthy were named delegates to the State Railroad Committee. The Keokuk Dubuque Railroad used John Plumbe's idea to trade land for railroad construction during 1848–49. Businesses and cities along the Mississippi River were desperate for a rail line because the steamboat companies cooperated to charge high rates for shipping.

When the Illinois Central Railroad began construction in Illinois, Lucius Langworthy, Jesse P. Farley, John Plumbe, Asa Horr and Platt Smith put

Jesse P. Farley's engine. *From the* Telegraph Herald *(Dubuque, Iowa)*.

forth a plan again for a transcontinental rail line through Dubuque. They organized the Dubuque and Pacific Railroad on April 28, 1853, with incorporation following on May 19, 1853. The Illinois Central reached Dunleith, Illinois (East Dubuque), in 1855. Construction on the Dubuque–Dyersville route began on October 1, 1855.

Construction of the rail line caused land prices to soar in addition to an explosion in the number of immigrants. In the 1850s, the population of Dubuque doubled, as did the profits for land speculators. A wood-burning locomotive, the *Dubuque*, from New Jersey, was ferried across the Mississippi. The *Jesse P. Farley* arrived shortly thereafter and made the first trip to Dyersville on May 11, 1857. Due to lack of rock under the rails, the train jumped the track three times. Train travel changed communities, people and geography. While these early trains could not claim speed or elegance, that soon changed. Before the railroad, a trip across the country cost about $1,000 to outfit. After the train, the same trip cost $150. While a stage could travel about ten miles per day, the train knew no such limitations. People who had never been more than a few miles from their birthplace now had the opportunity to see other regions.

The Panic of 1857, followed quickly by the Civil War from 1861 to 1865, slowed or stopped railroad construction. The Chicago, Iowa and Nebraska Railroad, the first rail line to cross Iowa, completed construction in 1867.

James Langworthy served on the executive committee and as a director of the Dubuque, St. Paul and St. Peter Railroad, along with F.E. Bissell and W.J. Barney. He also was the director of the J.L. Langworthy and Brothers' Bank. The Dubuque and Marine Insurance Company, of which James was a director, was the only insurance company in Iowa to make insured persons stockholders in the company. His sudden death on March 14, 1865, shocked Dubuque's residents. The city's longest living resident had been active to the day of his death. He had traveled to Monticello, Iowa, on business and stayed with his brother, William. He accepted an invitation to breakfast with Mr. J.L. Davenport, but a few minutes after his arrival, as he removed his overshoe, he slumped down and died. The official cause of death was listed as apoplexy (a term no longer used; it meant a state of unconsciousness and sudden death due to a cerebral hemorrhage or stroke). His brother and Mr. Davenport accompanied his body home on the train. The end of an era had come to the region. James Langworthy had been a pivotal influence in not only the city but also the state of Iowa and the United States. The railroads he had worked so determinedly to establish through Dubuque to the West and East had not yet happened, but the sound of the train whistle grew closer with each passing year.

Lucius Langworthy became a director in the Dubuque to Sioux City Railroad in 1859. He was also the president of the Dubuque Western Railroad and an original incorporator of the Pacific Railroad. In 1849, he sent a letter to Gilman Folsom, who practiced law in Iowa City and later was elected as a representative in Congress. Langworthy instructed Folsom to keep him informed of the "whys and wherefores" of railroad interests, as he was engaged in making surveys of the different routes to connect Dubuque with other points. He intended to have diagrams of these routes at Washington on the new maps as soon as possible.

The cost of railroad construction was more than even the wealthiest could manage. As an example, the track from Dubuque to Dyersville cost more than $36,000 per mile. Stock offerings helped to offset the cost, but eventually John Plumbe's plan to extend land grants to railroad companies, which could then sell the land, paid for the railroads. Proof of this solution to the cost of railroad construction came with the Railway Act of 1862, when Congress established "an act to aid in the construction of a railroad and telegraph line from the Missouri River to the Pacific Ocean and to secure to the Government the use of the same for postal, military and other purposes." The Railway Act also named Lucius Langworthy among those "together with commissioners to be appointed by the Secretary of Interior…are hereby created and erected into a body politic in deed and in law by the name, style and title of The Union Pacific Railroad Co." The original plans of Plumbe and the Langworthys were slowly coming to fruition.

GROWTH, CHANGE AND WAR

The Langworthy properties extended from Third Street to Delhi Street to Dodge Street to Julien (University) Avenue. Their homes formed an "L" pattern, with James's home on the corner of James and Langworthy Streets, Edward's home at the corner of Alpine and West Third Streets, Solon's home on Alpine Street and Lucius's home at the corner of Hill and Langworthy Streets. Today, only the home of Edward Langworthy remains in the family. The James Langworthy home was demolished, and the Lucius Langworthy home was extensively remodeled by new owner Titus Schmid. Solon's home became an apartment building but has since been restored.

Lucius Langworthy attended the log schools in Illinois while he worked on the family farm in Edwardsville. He wrote that corn was used as a medium of exchange: a yard of cloth equaled 4 bushels of corn, a cow equaled 95 bushels, a horse cost 362 bushels and a hog cost 50 bushels. Lucius then attended the first term of an academy taught by Dr. Lyman Beecher, the famous minister and abolitionist, in Jacksonville, Illinois. Following his education, he taught school in Bluffdale, Illinois, for two years prior to coming to Galena. He later wrote of the lead rush of 1827, "Accounts came sweeping down by each traveler of the great lead mines just opened up at Galena. Farms are sold, their stock and other valuables sold off at random. The old pioneers are on the wind again." He explained that the miners were often referred to as "suckers"—not because they lost everything to a scam, as modern readers might assume, but due to the fact that they arrived in the spring and left in the fall just as a species of fish known as suckers did. When the gold rush of 1849 hit the area, he wrote the following: "Gold! Gold! Gold! Oh thou mysterious Spirit, the root of all evil, but the top branches of all progress." He was referring here to the common belief among the early settlers and the miners before them that they were doing the work of the government in bringing civilization and, therefore, progress to the frontier. At a speech for the Dubuque Literary Institute on December 18, 1854, he described Dubuque as seen by his brother James and himself as they crossed the Mississippi River: "So wondrous wild, the whole might seem: the scenery of a fairy dream."

Lucius owned an interest in the *Dubuque Visitor*, Iowa's first newspaper. The first issue of the newspaper occurred on May 11, 1836. Lucius Langworthy involved himself in river traffic and trade by co-owning the steamboat *Heroine*. He also worked to improve Dubuque's harbor. His banking influence included serving as a director in the Miners' Bank of Dubuque. He was a firm advocate of railroads.

Lucius and Mary Francis Reeder of Cincinnati, Ohio, married on March 26, 1835, in St. Louis, Missouri. A few months later, in August, his brother Edward married Mary Francis's sister, Paulina. Lucius and Mary had two children: Lucius Bonaparte, who died in 1845, and Oscar Atlas (1838–1882), who survived to adulthood. Mary Reeder Langworthy died in 1839; Lucius later married Valeria Bemis in 1842. They had six children, with five surviving to adulthood: Ada Collier (1843–1919), Orrin (1846–1928), Ashmore (1848–1910), Ida (1852–1855), Lucius Hart (1854–1924) and Bernice McFadden (1848–1922). In 1849, they built a brick mansion on Hill Street. Lucius Langworthy had built the first frame house in Dubuque in 1834 on Rosedale Avenue. Their brick mansion facing Hill Street consisted of eighteen rooms, with a parlor and two living rooms on the main part of the first floor. A wing included a kitchen, a dining room and a pantry. The upper floor contained six bedrooms. The estate of twenty-five acres included a vast apple orchard that produced four to five hundred bushels of apples for storage in the cellar during the winter. The apples occupied the cellar space along with sides of beef on hooks hanging from the rafters, as well as bacon, hams and vegetables. Raspberries, currants and grapes grew on the estate and provided food for the family. A formal garden in the shape of a Maltese cross with a circular bed in the center was filled with flowers. The home entertained frequent guests, including President U.S. Grant and George Catlin, a famous artist.

Lucius wrote of an incident between Dr. John Stoddard, who was one of the early medical men in Dubuque, and Captain Edward White. Apparently, there existed an issue concerning a mining claim in Sullivan's Addition near the present Mount Pleasant Street. As a result, Dr. Stoddard shot and killed Captain White. Dr. Stoddard quickly exited Dubuque and escaped. While strolling through the woods, Lucius Langworthy came upon two rough stones that had been erected at the spot of the killing. He wrote that he then reflected on the vast changes that had occurred in Dubuque over the ensuing years, especially the fact that it was much more civilized with much less violence.

Gold walking stick with inlaid gold nugget given to Edward Langworthy by his brother Lucius. *Brad Chalmers.*

During the rush to the California gold fields, Lucius Langworthy, as had so many others, succumbed to gold fever. He headed to California but returned to Dubuque after a successful few years. While there, he sent his brother Edward an engraved gold walking cane head with a gold nugget attached. His mining skills were not limited to lead, it seems.

In a second lecture before the Dubuque Literary Institute on February 26, 1855, Lucius stated that immigration came into Dubuque from "all parts of the earth. German liberalism, New England Puritanism and Celtic nationalism all soon assimilated because there were a thousand interests and motives uniting to render it necessary for them to support each other." He continued to say that by 1836, when Dubuque remained a part of the Michigan Territory, there were about six thousand people living in Iowa—mostly along the Mississippi River. Since they believed that the soil in the mining districts could not be farmed, they were forced to import all their food stuff. Such incorrect beliefs, despite the proof of native planted cornfields that could be viewed in the entire area, left the early settlers vulnerable to starvation. His brother Solon helped to put this myth to rest by successfully plowing and planting his fields in Dubuque. In a bit of humor (or maybe not), Lucius mentioned that Dubuque rapidly became Democratic in politics. The reason for this, he said, was related to the legend of Lethe. Just as the waters around the mythical underworld conferred forgetfulness to those who entered, so had, he guessed, the waters of the Mississippi River infused people with forgetfulness, thus causing them to become Democrats!

Lucius Langworthy had a strong interest in education, as witnessed by his donation of land and thousands of dollars for Catherine Beecher, sister of Henry Ward Beecher and daughter of his early teacher, Lyman Beecher, to establish the Dubuque Female College at the corner of Seventeenth and Iowa Streets. His was, in fact, the single largest contribution for the erection of the college. The territorial governor of Michigan (Iowa being a part of Michigan Territory at this time) appointed Lucius Langworthy as the first sheriff of the county. He is also credited with supplying the name Iowa for the territory then part of Michigan. Since Lucius and his brother James had laid claim to most of the land on which the city of Dubuque had been built for $700, their real estate sales along with mining and other business enterprises made them the wealthiest citizens of Dubuque.

Lucius died on June 9, 1865. His passing so soon after James's death caused much grief in Dubuque. The *Dubuque Herald* reported, "He contributed in every way possible to the advancement of the interests of the Key City. These few words cannot tell of the enterprises which assisted in establishing the blessings of civilization in the wilds of the west, and developing the vast resources of Iowa." He was described by all who knew him as industrious and energetic, a man with a strict integrity. His obituary read, "We meet everywhere the evidence that he lived to good purpose and in death left the rich legacy of a worthy example."

Valeria Langworthy (wife of Lucius) composed "My First Impression of Dubuque" for her family. In this memoir, she explained that she had booked passage on the *Old Brazil*, a steamship owned and captained by Orrin Smith, husband of Mary Ann Langworthy. She arrived in Dubuque on April 8, 1842. She saw few homes other than her husband's and those of her brothers-in-law. She immediately set to cleaning with her maid, Ellen. The house had been vacant, so it was in desperate need. In 1843–44, the Mississippi River had flooded. She referred to it as the "big flood." Her father's family in Columbia Bolton in St. Charles County, Missouri, had been flooded out of their home. As a result, they moved to Dubuque. Her father, Nathan Bemis, traveled to Maryland, where he stayed until spring to complete some business. Valeria found the winter of 1844 to be very grueling, as it was quite cold and she was very unused to cold and snow, having lived in Maryland and Missouri. She wrote that "my grandmother sat by the fireplace in a coat, hat and bed comforter." This first home (more of a miner's cabin), located along Couler Avenue (Highway 3 N) at Langworthy Hollow (Kaufman Avenue), lacked many comforts. The chimney, according to Valeria, was so badly built that she could poke her finger through it. Cooking and baking had to be done on a small stove. Lucius brought deer, small game, quail and prairie chickens for the family. They had purchased supplies in St. Louis before leaving, so they had sugar, flour, bacon, coffee and "a barrel of mackerel." Plums and blackberries supplemented their diet along with wild strawberries that, she said, covered a meadow near the house. In the spring, a small stream flowed past her father's house (now Kaufman Avenue), sometimes to a depth of four feet depending on the snowmelt. She greatly admired the Canterbury bell and scarlet cardinal flowers that filled the open sandy areas between Eagle Point and the Fifth Ward School (Audubon School).

Mrs. Langworthy recalled that typhus claimed many lives. Typhus is rare in the United States today, but in areas of poor hygiene or poverty, it still presents a danger. Typhus is caused by a bacterial infection resulting from a bite from fleas, ticks, mites or lice. It was most usually transmitted to humans via fleas on rats. Wherever grain or food was stored, there were rats. During Mrs. Langworthy's time, however, they believed that typhus resulted "by upturning of the rich soil." Unfortunately, she also mentioned a once beautiful stream that the miners washed in and into which they dumped their garbage and other refuse. Such practices only increased the likelihood of disease.

A reception and lawn party on June 16, 1905, commemorated the fifty-sixth anniversary of Solon and Julia Langworthy's house. Julia Langworthy, who was eighty-two years old, attended. She remembered coming to the lead mines as a child in 1833 with her father, Myron Patterson, and her mother. They had traveled on the steamer *Don Juan* to Rock Island, where cholera prevented them from leaving the boat. They continued on to Galena. That fall, they traveled to Peru by oxcart and ferry. Her father blazed his own trail through the wilderness. Upon reaching the DuBuque Mines, he discovered that the lumber he had bought and stored there had been stolen. He used logs sawed at Fort Crawford (Prairie du Chien) and floated down the Mississippi River to build a cabin. Located close to the Timber Diggings (Durango), they met many miners, some of whom were quite ill. Julia and her mother nursed the sick miners with homemade soup made from rabbits and squirrels, as well as provided them a clean place to rest. All cooking had to be accomplished outdoors. When it rained, an umbrella held over the fire kept it from going out. Julia's parents sent her to Dubuque to attend school. She boarded with Mrs. Gehon, who lived in the house built by James Langworthy at Twelfth and Iowa Streets. Mr. King taught classes in a building where the Dubuque Club once stood at Ninth and Locust Streets. The building used by Mr. King had been the home of

Francis and Mrs. Gehon, early settlers. The house, located in Peru, was cut in half and then transported to Dubuque.

At the age of seventeen, Julia Patterson married Solon Langworthy on April 20, 1840. Dubuque became their permanent home in 1848. The author of Julia Langworthy's obituary wrote admiringly of her accomplishments on the frontier: "She excelled at the homely arts of the quilting bee, of homemade soap, tallow candles, rendering of lard, care of meats, the making of rag rugs and the upbuilding of the primitive church (she was a lifelong member of the First Congregational Church in Dubuque). All the while rearing a family."

Of their new home on the bluff, she fondly remembered the road that ran through the tall grass in front of the house and the sound of the wind as it blew through the treeless countryside. It was the custom of the Indians to burn off the landscape to encourage game to move into the area. Today, the tree-covered bluffs appear to us as if they had always been that way, but that is not the case. Julia continued her walk down memory lane with recollections of hazel brush thickets at her doorstep and the planting of fourteen and a half acres of trees and orchards. Their home (now on Alpine Street) had been built by Chauncey G. Laurence, with woodwork, doors and windows all made in Dubuque. The bricks for the home came from the Langworthy brickyard, as they did for all the Langworthy homes. The support posts for the spacious veranda came from forests near Dubuque. Since too few carpenters existed in Dubuque at this early date, Solon called a "bee" to finish the home (this meant that neighbors, friends and relatives came to assist in the finishing of a project—in this case the Langworthy home). Julia remarked that "Dr. Finley was most helpful with a hammer and saw!" On September 1, 1858, the Langworthys held a jubilee at their home in honor of the laying of the Atlantic cable. The home saw many family festivities throughout the years, as they viewed the growing city, the river and the road to the west from their veranda.

Mrs. Julia Langworthy joined and worked tirelessly with the Mount Vernon Ladies Association, whose purpose was to save and restore George Washington's home. While the men in Congress refused to believe in this cause, the women raised $200,000 to purchase the home and two hundred acres in 1858. Today, the association operates Mount Vernon with no government support.

Mrs. Horace Poole, daughter of Julia Langworthy, donated funds to construct double iron gates for the Mount Pleasant Home in Dubuque. In June 1918, a dedication celebration featuring the newly installed gates

The home of Solon and Julia Langworthy. *Photo by author.*

honored the contributions made by Mrs. Langworthy as a founding member of the Mount Pleasant Home.

Solon Langworthy had a gas house built in a field near their home so he could manufacture resin gas. He had purchased the technology for the process in Brooklyn, New York. Resin gas begins as rosin obtained from pine trees or stumps and some plants. Homes and businesses, as well as urban areas, used the resin gas for illumination. Rosin must be first melted and then passed through red hot coke and gasified. This raw resin gas was then separated from the resin oil, cooled and passed through a sodium hydroxide solution to remove the carbon dioxide in the gas. The resin oil was then fed back into the production process and recycled. Since no sulfurous acid existed in resin gas, fewer odors resulted. It was also brighter, cleaner and cheaper than coal gas. At first, rosin coming from North America cost much less than coal, but eventually that changed. As coal became cheaper, rosin increased in cost. By the end of the nineteenth century, resin gas had been replaced. All of the Langworthy homes were lit by Solon's resin gasworks, as were many businesses during the early years of Dubuque.

John and Bernice McFadden (daughter of Lucius Langworthy) built an Arts and Crafts–style home on West Third Street in Dubuque near her father's home. The home displayed an arched entryway, second-story bay windows and a roof of rounded Spanish tiles. The interior boasts beamed ceilings, paneled walls and a marble fireplace. John McFadden sat on the faculty of the Presbyterian Seminary in Dubuque as a professor of oratory.

Lucius H. Langworthy (1854–1924), son of Lucius and Valeria, married Carrie Glover, whose parents lived on Fenelon Place. Their grand wedding on June 6, 1877, at the Congregational Church attracted many spectators, some of whom watched the ceremony from the balcony. Mr. Glover, a well-known Main Street merchant, spared no expense for the wedding reception

Mount Pleasant's iron gates. *Photo by author.*

held at the family home. Each table displayed a pyramid of coconut macaroons along with white wedding cakes. The wedding date of June 6 held particular significance for the bride's family, as her parents married on the same date and also had arrived in Dubuque on June 6. They had two children, Caroline Valeria (1854–1924) and Henry Glover (1880–1961). Lucius Jr. moved to Omaha due to his business, but his wife and daughter remained in Dubuque since she was pregnant with their second child. When he returned to visit his family in October, Carrie insisted on traveling with him to Omaha rather than staying in Dubuque. Against the advice of Dr. Hill—who was not only her physician but also a close personal friend—they embarked for Omaha. Dr. Hill accompanied them, but when they reached Clinton, Iowa, Carrie went into labor, so they could go no farther. A baby boy arrived on November 1, and all seemed well. Lucius Jr. departed for Omaha with his two-year-old daughter, and Carrie's mother arrived in Clinton. After several days, Carrie became severely ill. Her mother called for a doctor, but nothing could be done to save her. Lucius hastily returned to Clinton. She died on November 12, 1880, with her husband at her side.

The baby boy grew up to follow in his ancestor's shoes by becoming a medical doctor. Dr. Henry Langworthy, grandson of Lucius and great-grandson of Dr. Stephen Langworthy, practiced medicine for forty-five years in Dubuque, retiring in 1945. The *Dubuque Telegraph Herald* of August 23, 1908, published an article titled "Medical Men of the Early Days," written by Dr. Henry Langworthy. Interestingly, he included Dr. Hill, who was most definitely not a man but rather a woman graduate of the University of Michigan Medical School, president of the Women's Suffrage Association and the very doctor who delivered him. He went on to write of his grandfather Dr. Stephen Langworthy, "He enjoyed the confidence of the whole community and was called to do surgery and consultations in serious cases at great distances. His companions described him as advanced for his day and the complete opposite of his sons as a highly trained physician, not a businessman." Dr. Henry Langworthy also chaired the Dubuque Centennial Association celebration of August 6–12, 1933. For the occasion, he wrote a four-act historical play featuring local talent commemorating the history of Dubuque. The *Telegraph Herald and Times Journal* of January 29, 1933, described the upcoming festivity as a "veritable Mardi Gras of entertainment."

Another Langworthy to pursue a career in medicine, Dr. Mitchell Langworthy, became a specialist and bone surgeon in Seattle, Washington. He was the grandson of Solon Massey Langworthy. During World War I, he served as an orthopedic surgeon at Base Hospital no. 23 in France. In a letter written to his father, Dr. Solon Massey Langworthy Jr., he stated that he was working with a "good group of men" and that several were from Iowa. Tragically, a patient shot and killed both Dr. Langworthy and his surgical nurse before turning the gun on himself in their consulting room on October 7, 1929. No reason was given other than he was determined to have become "insane as a result of a railroad tunnel accident."

Edward and Paulina Langworthy built the famous Octagon House on West Third Street in Dubuque in 1856. Designed by John Francis Rague, who copied the design from a building in Washington, D.C., the home's walls are of double brick from the Langworthy brickyard, with a foundation of native limestone. Its supportive beams are of hand-hewn oak and walnut. The joists are held in place by square nails and wooden dowels. The marble for the fireplace mantels arrived from Italy, and the house was equipped with gas lighting. The home follows the "fad in the 1850s of Orson S. Fowler's Octagonal mode of Building." The house has a columned entry with a T-shaped entry hall and a central double staircase. The living room is on one side of the staircase and the library on the other. The second floor has six bedrooms. All but two of them have angled walls. Angular tall bay windows supply sunlight to the living and dining rooms. Bronze chandeliers with gold leaf illuminate the parlor. A large central windowed cupola encloses the upper portions of the chimneys. Two long interior walls define the long side of the stair hall and contain the fireplace and lower portions of the chimneys. The grand parlor, with its two ceiling-high mirrors, stretches the full length of the first floor. The parlor's large, rosewood piano had been given to the Presbyterian church, but when it no longer wanted it, they scheduled it for the dump. Edward Langworthy Chalmers rescued it along with a Lincoln rocker. The parlor has been kept as it was in 1857. The floral carpeting in the room is an exact duplicate of the original. The Alexander Smith Carpet Company took the job as a challenge. There were forty-eight different shades of colors needed to reproduce the carpet. Other than a slight difference in the size of the roses, it is indistinguishable from the original. The plush velvet draperies and upholstery have also been replaced with replicas. A grandfather clock from 1832 that once stood in the parlor was donated to the Carnegia Stout Public Library.

Originally, there were three rooms in a row separated by partitions hanging from the ceiling. When the family held dances, the partitions could be lifted for more room. The August 24, 1914 issue of the *Dubuque Telegraph Herald* noted in an article about old Dubuque homes that even all the window panes

Langworthy's grandfather clock. *Photo by author.*

remained original, with only one exception. To furnish the home, Edward Langworthy traveled by horse and buggy to Rockford, Illinois, where the nearest railroad station existed, and then took the train to New York. All the interior furnishings purchased there had to be shipped to Dubuque by way of the Atlantic Ocean and the Mississippi River.

A second, smaller octagonal house built in the 1850s by Mr. Eichorn at 1672 Central Avenue was torn down in 1932. The building, originally used as a residence, became a machine shop before being razed and replaced by Lentz Monuments. Davenport, Iowa, was a hub of activity for octagon house construction. There once existed six or seven such houses there, but most have been destroyed. Des Moines, Iowa, also saw a boom in octagon house construction, but these were only one-story homes, of which several survive. Several reasons for the construction of these houses include the idea that they were tornado resistant and that contractors believed that ninety-degree corners harbored ghosts. A more practical consideration was that with only one exterior wall, rooms were easier and cheaper to heat.

In August 1885, Edward and Paulina Langworthy celebrated their fiftieth wedding anniversary in grand style at their residence. They had married on August 3, 1835, at Peru in Edward's former cabin. Five hundred invitations went out for the anniversary celebration. The veranda and lawns were lit up with Chinese lanterns and decorated with flags. Carriages came and went during the festivities, which lasted from 7:00 p.m. to 10:00 p.m. The Wunderlich Orchestra provided music for the enjoyment of the guests. The invitations stated that no gifts were necessary, but many ignored that request. The H.L. Stout family gave the couple one dozen gold after-dinner spoons. Mrs. John Hancock sent a lyre-shaped flower arrangement of roses, jasmine and goldenrod.

One interesting story told of Edward involved the transport of gold earned from his mining endeavors to a bank in St. Louis. He had placed the gold in a chest that was so heavy it had to be loaded on the steamboat with a trolley. When Edward checked on his trunk a few days later, he found someone had augered a hole in the bottom of the chest. Had he waited another day to check on his baggage, the gold would have been no more. Edward Langworthy died on January 4, 1893. He was the last of the brothers to die. Mathias M. Ham said of his death, "The passing of the Langworthy brothers marks an epoch in the history of the State of Iowa."

An additional commentary on Edward Langworthy spoke to his integrity and loyalty. During the construction of the new capitol building in Iowa City, begun in 1840, a controversy involving Acting Commissioner Chauncey

The home of Edward and Paulina Langworthy. *Photo by author.*

Swan caused Edward Langworthy to accuse his fellow commissioners of excluding evidence that would have been beneficial to Swan. An investigation in 1840 by those who accused Swan of corruption vindicated him of the mishandling of funds. Langworthy and the other supporters of Swan said that the accusations "smelled of boiling cauliflower."

Frances Langworthy Gibbs (1841–1926), daughter of Edward and Paulina, attended Dubuque Female College at Seventeenth and Iowa Streets and Willard's in New York. The Emma Willard School, founded in 1821 by women's rights advocate Emma Willard, remains today a highly ranked university preparatory boarding and day school for young women. It was the first higher education institution in the United States for girls. The school's philosophy states: " Every young woman who attends Emma Willard will be encouraged to develop fully in all areas of her life, as a strong intellectual in a variety of disciplines, as a practitioner of her chosen passions, as a social member of her community and as a responsible global citizen in her future."

This description certainly described Frances Langworthy Gibbs. She belonged to the Dubuque Women's Club and Daughters of the American Revolution and worked on many local charity events. In 1914, during World

Left: Paulina Reeder Langworthy. *Brad Chalmers*.

Right: Francis "Frannie" Langworthy, daughter of Edward and Paulina Langworthy. *Brad Chalmers*.

War I, she organized the American Christmas Ship to send gifts, toys, candy and clothing to children in war-torn Europe. In 1902, she traveled to Los Angeles to attend the National Women's Club Convention as a delegate from Iowa. As a member of the club, she campaigned for child labor laws and worked locally for better sanitation by cleaning alleys and demanding that the public cup at drinking fountains be abolished. The Women's Club even hired a horticulturist to assist citizens with plantings to beautify the city, as well as cleaned playgrounds, assembled Christmas baskets for the needy and fought juvenile delinquency. The club also played a prominent role in the development of Eagle Point Park and the Hillcrest Baby Fold. It even gifted the City of Dubuque the bluff lots west of Bluff Street to Hill Street after it had restored them to their natural condition and removed all the billboards that had littered the hillside. The civic contributions of Frances Gibbs and her colleagues continued to benefit Dubuque for many years.

Frances Langworthy married Adrian Gibbs of Ohio in 1863. His grandmother had been a member of the Stuart family of Scotland. The kings of England James I and II and Charles I and II belonged to the Stuart family line. (Remember that Solon Langworthy said their ancestors had played a major role in the execution of Charles I.) Adrian moved to the area in 1855. Adrian's cousin Mary Newberry Adams and her husband, Austin Adams, arrived in Dubuque a year earlier. Austin Adams (of the same family as Samuel Adams and two presidents) and Mary Newberry Adams became leading Dubuque citizens. Mrs. Adams supported the suffragette movement and was one of the founders of the Northern Iowa Suffrage Society. Their son, Eugene, bought a partnership in the Langworthy–Adams Iron Works. Today, the Adams Company remains a prominent business in Dubuque.

Adrian Gibbs's brother Pierre, who was a civil engineer, as well as his mother and sister, followed him Dubuque. They then lived in Dunleith (East Dubuque). He managed the businesses of C.H. Merry. Captain Merry operated a ferry, a grain elevator, a coal supply company, riverboats and the Illinois Central Railroad station. He also owned the Merchants Dispatch, a freight forwarding service. The Captain Merry mansion, built in 1866, demonstrated his wealth. The mansion in East Dubuque is currently a site for Airbnb. While working for Merry, Adrian Gibbs inaugurated the method of transporting grain in bulk on barges from the Upper Mississippi River to New Orleans and on to Liverpool, England. After Adrian and Frances married, they lived in Dubuque on Iowa Street. He opened his own business as a grain buyer and commission merchant. He temporarily moved to Leadville, Colorado, where he worked for the Denver and South Park Railroad. He died on December 14, 1896. At that time, Frances moved into the Edward Langworthy home with her sister Pauline Rood and niece, Eleanor.

On June 10, 1885, Edward Langworthy, along with Chandler Childs and Alexander Simplot, founded the Dubuque County Early Settlers' Association to recognize those members of the community who had played a role in the founding of Dubuque County. Membership of a dollar applied only to men, as women were admitted for free. The thirty-sixth annual meeting of the Early or Old Settlers' Association was held at Twin Springs in Center Township, Dubuque County. More than five thousand people attended. The Great Western Railroad ran a special excursion train for the celebration. The train made six round trips, with the coach cars crowded each time, according to the *Dubuque Daily Telegraph*. Athletic events, food tents, beer tents and a dance contributed to the festive atmosphere. The Honorable J.J. McCarthy delivered the opening speech emphasizing the purpose of the day: "A perfect summer's day here amid the giant trees, refreshing shade, huge hills and rocks, the gently flowing Maquoketa (Little Maquoketa River), the gushing sparkling twin springs away from habitation, removed from the crowded city, workshops and farm. Here in this wild, romantic spot designed by nature as a lovely rural retreat; how appropriate a place for a meeting of the pioneer settlers who survived to tell the story of days gone by." Those honored at this remembrance included a special tribute to the legacy of Stephen Langworthy.

Solon Langworthy's story continued just as noteworthy as those of his brothers. After his discharge from the army in 1834 following the Black Hawk War, Solon Langworthy returned to St. Charles, Illinois, with Ezra Overall and his cousins William and Jesse Moureing, only to learn that his brother-in-law Jacob Williams had died of cholera. Solon stayed in St. Charles to assist his sister Laura in settling the estate. The lure of a fortune in lead was irresistible, so Solon boarded the steamboat *Olive Branch* for Galena, where he met his sister Maria and her husband, Captain Daniel Smith Harris. Harris had come to Galena as a clerk for Dr. Moses Meeker in 1824. They continued to Dubuque on Harris's boat, *Jo Daviess*, named for the county in Illinois that was, in turn, named in honor of Major Joseph Hamilton Daviess, who died at the Battle of Tippecanoe in 1811. They visited his brothers at their mining cabin at Langworthy Hollow. The area was along the southern portion of Couler Valley (Highway 3 N), specifically Kaufmann Avenue and East Twenty-Second Street.

Solon Langworthy, known as the first man to plow land in Iowa, farmed sixty acres north of Dubuque for his brother Lucius. In 1837, he owned the steamboat *Brazil* with Orrin Smith, his brother-in-law. They bought the steamer with money made from lead mining. Solon had carried $22,000 in his belt on his journey to Cincinnati, where the *Brazil* was built. On its first voyage, April 1, 1837, it carried the lumber needed to build the Le Claire House, the first hotel in Davenport. Unfortunately, on its third or fourth voyage, the boat sank. With no insurance, it was a total loss. In the winter of 1838, Solon traveled to St. Louis on horseback. Near St. Louis in Green County, he met H.L. Massey, his cousin. Massey had left the mining camp at Dubuque in 1835. They continued on to St. Louis, where they bought a wagon and four horses. After loading the wagon with clothing and blankets, Massey headed north to the Snake Hollow Mines (Potosi, Wisconsin), while Solon went on to Cincinnati. Solon bought more goods there and used them to establish a store in Potosi, Wisconsin, to supply the miners. About this time, Solon met Julia Patterson, who was living in Peru, Iowa, with her father, Myron Patterson. The town of Peru at the confluence of the Little Maquoketa River and the Mississippi River resulted from an act of Congress in 1836 that laid out the township and set aside a section of land for a city. Peru grew to include stores, hotels, homes and businesses, but the harbor at the Dubuque Mines proved superior, so Peru never developed into a city. Today, it no longer exists, as the site is covered by the Dubuque John Deere Works.

Solon, while not impressed with Peru, was struck by Julia. He wrote, "But in my judgment Julia L.P. was at the time all there was in the county or town which was of interest to me and our friendship was unbroken." They were married in Lafayette, Wisconsin (near Potosi), on April 20, 1840. In 1848, they took up permanent residence in Dubuque.

Solon was the only Langworthy brother to serve in no political office, focusing instead on his businesses. He did run for the position of delegate to the Wisconsin State Constitution Convention but was defeated. Of his defeat, he said, "Despite my defeat, the state and country are yet safe." He entered the mercantile business with his cousin H.L. Massey. Their business supplied fruits and vegetables for Civil War soldiers at Camp Franklin (Camp Union) north of Dubuque.

During the Civil War, Iowa's Governor Samuel J. Kirkwood supported the Union, pledging "his own money to equip volunteers for the Union army." In Dubuque, a training center was established to "house recruits as regiments were filled, and to turn those civilians into soldiers for the war." The first training center was Camp Union "because the area had been used for drills by the Union Brigade, one of Dubuque's earlier volunteer companies." Located near the Mississippi River near current-day Rhomberg Street, "it opened in August, 1861, and served initially as a recruiting center for the Ninth and Twelfth Iowa Volunteer Infantry. Within a month there were 600 volunteers at the camp under the military discipline of Col. William B. Allison."

"There were ten barracks with outdoor cooking and eating sections, water and bathing facilities, and ample food. Col. J.K. Graves served as quartermaster at the camp and gave out rations and blankets." Dubuquers lent blankets when it was learned that many soldiers lacked bedding. "The Governor's Greys of Dubuque was the first company to volunteer, shoulder their muskets and go off to the war under General Francis J. Herron of Dubuque. [Herron was captured and exchanged for a Confederate soldier during the war and later became a lawyer in New Orleans.]" Sketching scenes of the war for *Harper's Weekly* was Alexander Simplot, a Dubuque native born in 1837, who accompanied General Ulysses S. Grant. When he became ill, Simplot returned to Dubuque to live. Many of his early sketches can be seen at the Center for Dubuque History, Loras College. These sketches provide insight into early Dubuque society. This is the same Alexander Simplot who had attended the short-lived Alexander College in Dubuque.

The Union Camp closed in December 1861, partly due to anti-war sentiment in Dubuque and poor organization. The camp reopened in July 1862 "under the name of Camp Franklin, housing the 21st, 27th, 32nd, and 38th regiments. All 120 men of the 21st regiment were Dubuquers and Captain Swivel was their leader. Many had enlisted to avoid the draft." Many businessmen were concerned about the river trade being damaged by the "Union cause." Because of Dubuque's location, J.K. Graves built a hospital at the camp to treat the numerous wounded and sick soldiers. "During the fall of 1862, outbreaks of typhoid, measles and other diseases occurred, causing eleven deaths and more than 200 sick men. Also, because of bitter feelings between two German-American companies, there was a murder at the camp. Sick soldiers were cared for by the Soldiers Aid Society and the Dubuque Women's Society [founded by Dubuquer Mrs. Julia L. Langworthy, who was an energetic relief worker during the war]." The hospital was initially run by the Sisters of Charity, BVM. The hospital was later torn down, with a boys' boarding school, known as the Columbia Academy (Loras College), built in its place.

Governor Kirkwood visited the camp in October 1862 as complaints about patient care surfaced at his office. "A report at Camp Franklin indicated that 193 men had been admitted to the camp hospital, 163 had returned to duty, seven were convalescing, one had been discharged, eight had died and fourteen were still in the hospital quite ill." Apparently, poor cooking methods were blamed for the complaints. There was even talk of secession in Dubuque as the predominantly Democrat Dubuque did not support Republican President Lincoln or the war. For these reasons, the governor closed the camp. The buildings were dismantled and sold at an auction in January 1863 for $1,564.

Solon Langworthy enlisted in the Twenty-Seventh Regiment of Iowa Volunteers during the Civil War in the fall of 1862. He was commissioned an officer on October 3, 1862. He was one of 952 men who enlisted. Captain George S. Pierce mustered Solon into service in the Nineteenth United States Infantry, where he served as regimental quartermaster. There were measles in the camp, so the men were transferred to Fort Snelling in Minnesota. While there, he went to Mille Lacs Lake, Minnesota, to supervise government payments to the natives, while the other soldiers remained in camp. Following that assignment, he was ordered to Prairie du Chien and then by rail to Madison, Wisconsin; Chicago; Cairo, Illinois; and Memphis,

Tennessee. In Memphis, he joined General Sherman's army. Following skirmishes near Waterford, Mississippi, during which the Confederate soldiers retreated, Solon was captured at Holly Springs, Mississippi. Major General Earl Van Dorn of the Confederate army had launched a surprise attack against the supply depot at Holly Springs, destroying $1.5 million in supplies intended for General Grant. Held as a prisoner of war at Holly Springs, Solon was later exchanged for Confederate prisoners.

Solon's wife, Julia, assisted other local women making clothing for the Union troops in the Globe Building, located at the corner of Fifth and Main Streets. She visited her husband in 1863 while his regiment was in Memphis. Instead of additional personal clothing in her bags, she brought much-needed medical supplies and other useful items for the soldiers. She was also on the executive board of the Northern Iowa Sanitary Fair, held in Dubuque in 1864 at the city hall. They had various activities, including the German Band, a children's activity area and an auction. Mrs. Shiras donated a vase that sold for $40, and four handmade handkerchiefs donated by Mrs. John T. Hancock and Mrs. G.B. Grosvenor commanded $42 at auction. Amazingly, the fair donated $81,000 to assist the Union soldiers. Her charity continued after the Civil War, when she personally attended the graves of veterans of that war in Linwood Cemetery and placed flowers on each one.

Frances Langworthy Poole, a daughter of James and Agnes Langworthy, worked as president of the Dubuque Volunteers Aid Society during the Civil War. The group collected and sent boxes of supplies to the Twelfth Regiment Iowa Volunteers. These supplies included five comforters, two cushions, one and a half dozen towels, one and a half dozen shirts, blackberry jam, preserved cherries, tomatoes, peaches, gooseberries, pin cushions, wine, pickles, barley, linen and other items. They also sponsored a knitting bee to make socks and mittens for the soldiers. The following is a portion of the poem "The Stocking" that was read by the makers of the socks as they knitted: "By the fireside cozily seated; With spectacles riding her nose; The lively old lady is knitting; A wonderful pair of hose; She pities the shivering soldier; Who is out in the pelting storm; And busily plies her needles to keep him hearty and warm; And now while beginning to narrow; She thinks of the Maryland mud; And wonders if ever the stocking; Will wade to the ankle in blood."

In 1864, Solon left the military and returned to Dubuque. Solon and Julia had six children, five of whom survived to adulthood. In 1856, they had built a Greek Revival home. It is unusual because the back of the house faces Langworthy Street today. The area once had no other homes, so the front

Solon Langworthy's Civil War trunk. *Photo by author.*

The Langworthy family Masquerade Party. *Langworthy scrapbook, Center for Dubuque History, Loras College.*

of the home, with its columns and porches, overlooked the city and the river. The estate possessed orchards, a herd lot and a large garden, with a smaller front garden surrounded by a gated fence and greenhouse. A vast front lawn with huge shade trees fronted on the road to Center Grove. Solon's gasworks, built on the property, illuminated all the Langworthy homes—the first in the city. Solon and Julia's annual New Year's Eve parties opened their home to the enjoyment of the town's residents with huge galas.

LANGWORTHY INFLUENCE
AT HOME AND BEYOND

*I*n 1879, Solon and Julia Langworthy sold several parcels of land to the City of Dubuque so Third Street could be widened. Later, in 1891, his widow gave the city land to construct both Alpine and Langworthy Streets. The Solon and Julia Langworthy property was subdivided into six lots when she died in 1907. W.J. Ewe bought and then sold the Solon Langworthy house to August and Emma Klein in 1934. They had it divided into apartments. Jeremy Wainwright purchased the home in 1998 and began an extensive restoration. It is a bed-and-breakfast at present.

Solon and his wife participated in many philanthropic ventures, as did all the Langworthy family members. In his will, Dr. John Finley left his property, valued at $80,000, for the purposes of a hospital. Edward Langworthy chaired a committee of citizens, including Solon Langworthy, to discuss the establishment of a second hospital in Dubuque. The committee decided to buy the entire Finley Homestead for use as a temporary 40-bed hospital. A fundraising campaign for the renovation of the building and equipment began immediately. The glass-walled cupola became the surgery since it had the best light. The first patients arrived at Finley Hospital in April 1890. Today, Finley Hospital is a 126-bed hospital affiliated with Unity Point Health.

Mrs. Julia Langworthy and Mrs. James Langworthy played prominent roles in the founding of the Home for the Friendless as members of the board of directors. The home housed women and children who had no means of support or had been orphaned. Fifty-three local women established a corporation with $50,000 in 1874. Each woman had two shares of stock. The number of residents soon outgrew the original home on Hill Street, so Mr. and Mrs. Jeffrey Griffith, a prominent Dubuque attorney, donated their mansion and two acres of land. Mr. and Mrs. Griffith both left $5,000 in their wills for the home. The State of Iowa contributed an additional $5,000 for maintenance. In 1877, the directors delivered a horse-drawn wagon filled with shoes, dry goods and clothing for the residents. Every year, the board of directors held a Charity Ball for the financial support of the Home for the Friendless. It was the only time the board requested any funds from the locality. Women were hired to run the facility, which included cattle, chickens, orchards, grapevines and huge gardens. Residents who were able worked there. In 1891, a "house man" was hired to maintain the furnace and outdoor work. The first fifty-one residents included thirty-nine homeless children. On January 2, 1914, the Home for the Friendless officially became Mount Pleasant Home. In 1957, children no longer stayed at Mount Pleasant due to changes in Iowa law regarding the care of children and a foster parent system. In 1979, the gardens were abandoned as interest in them no longer existed. In 1986, male residents were admitted for the first time. Mount Pleasant continues to offer an assisted-living option for thirty-nine residents in Dubuque on Mount Pleasant Street.

Mrs. Julia Langworthy, a member of the Congregational Church, joined Mrs. Maude Marshall in singing "Radiant Morn" and "Hark, Hark, My Soul" for a special service on November 14, 1897. The sermon on current events from a religious standpoint included "Lovejoy an Apostle of Emancipation for Slaves," "Marcus Whitman Who Saved Oregon for the U.S." and "Cuba's Struggles." She was also a member of the Horticultural Society. The society sponsored a three-day convention in Dubuque in 1885.

Mrs. Julia Langworthy traveled to Kirksville, Missouri, to seek remedy for health ailments. There she saw Dr. Andrew Taylor, who practiced osteopathy. Dr. Taylor had been a surgeon in the Union army during the Civil War but became disenchanted with the treatments of the era that relied on arsenic, strychnine, mercury and foxglove—all poisons. After the Civil War, his wife and four children died of spinal meningitis, and he concluded that modern medicine was ineffective. He began a practice devoted to "rational medical therapy and manipulation of the musculoskeletal system and surgery with sparing use of drugs." He was one of the first doctors to promote preventative medicine.

Julia's support of osteopathy and preventative medicine had an impact on their son Solon Massey Langworthy Jr., who graduated in 1904 from the

Mount Pleasant (Home for the Friendless). *Photo by author.*

Palmer School of Chiropractic in Davenport, Iowa. He and fellow graduates Oakley Smith and Minora Paxson immediately founded the American School of Chiropractic and Nature Cure in Cedar Rapids, Iowa. They offered the first structured two-year curriculum for chiropractic, as well as the first professional journal of chiropractic, *The Backbone*. The competition with the Palmer School was not welcomed. When Langworthy and his associates attempted to secure a licensure procedure for chiropractic in Minnesota,

D.D. Palmer and his son met with the governor and persuaded him not to sign the legislation. The controversy continued into the twentieth century. Even today there is controversy regarding the contributions of Langworthy to the field of chiropractic.

While the Langworthys usually focused on local and national issues, international events did not escape the attention of the family. In 1880, Dubuque welcomed Charles Stewart Parnell and John Dillon with a guard of honor and a reception. Solon Langworthy was a member of the committee responsible for organizing the affair. Parnell, a leader of the Irish Parliamentary Party demanding Irish Home Rule, and Dillon, who was also a member of the movement and a supporter of Parnell, arrived in McGregor, Iowa, where they were met by the Dubuque Committee. Members of the committee accompanied them on the train to Dubuque. The honor guard escorted them from the depot to the hotel. A lavish reception with decorations and Colonel D.J. Davis as marshal of the celebration welcomed them to Dubuque, where the mayor and aldermen extended the city's hospitality.

The Watson and Langworthy (Solon) Company owned land near Tacoma, Washington. As Solon became aware that the forests of northern Wisconsin could not last forever, he protected their financial assets by securing future lumber interests in the West. Solon also owned the building housing Merrill's Wire Fence Factory at Iowa and Second Streets. A fire engulfed the building in March 1878, destroying most of the structure and heavily damaging the contents. Luckily, the Merrill family, who lived upstairs, as well as the workers, escaped with their lives. It was almost impossible to find a business venture during the 1900s in which the Langworthys had not secured an interest.

The DuBuque Mines, first visited by the Langworthy brothers, had become a city of brick buildings, reading rooms, lyceums, a Thespian Society and seminaries of learning. The lyceum movement began in Massachusetts in the 1820s as opportunities for those who attended for self-improvement through lectures on literary, scientific and moral topics. The Dubuque's Young Men's Literary Association sponsored German revolutionary and Union general Carl Schurz and abolitionist and suffragist Frederick Douglass, a former slave who "stole himself from bondage," as speakers. Douglass spoke three times in Dubuque between 1866 and 1870. St. Raphael's Cathedral Lyceum Debating Society was founded in 1876. The newspapers, exuding pride, referred to Dubuque as the "Athens of the West."

On Sunday, June 6, 1886, Solon Langworthy took his relatives Mrs. James Langworthy and Mrs. D.G. Scott for a pleasure ride to the old

Langworthy Homestead past the fairgrounds in Couler Valley (Highway 3 N). Later that same day, while he visited Mrs. Scribe Harris, Solon suffered a stroke, leaving him partially paralyzed. He died at home on June 7, 1886, and was buried at Linwood Cemetery, Dubuque, Iowa. Solon Langworthy, in his old age, once described his life as follows: "My life has been spent in industrial pursuits, embracing farming, mining, merchandising, banking, dealing in real estate and lumber. Moderate success has never crowned my labors. I have sustained innumerable losses, two or three of which left me almost dependent and yet by dint of industry and economy I have recovered without material aid from friends."

In June 1932, Dubuque Senior High School presented an assembly honoring Dubuque pioneers. Mary Langworthy Bunting (daughter of Solon Langworthy) was the honored guest, as she was the last surviving member in the second generation of the Langworthy family. The celebration culminated Pioneer Week at the high school, with a dance performed by June Kirk and Eleona Appel titled "Two Little Girls in Blue" that had been popular in pioneer days. When they had finished, Peter Seippel, president of the student council, delivered a speech on the purpose of Pioneer Week. Marshall School on Rhomberg Avenue presented an additional program in 1932 to honor the region's pioneers. The students reenacted a day at the Fifth Ward School of 1850 by completing assignments of that era. During music class, they sang the songs of the period, and at recess, they played the same games the youngsters of 1850 might have enjoyed. During an assembly, they impersonated James Langworthy, General Caleb Booth, General George W. Jones and Joseph Rhomberg for their guests. In the evening, the school held a dance featuring the students demonstrating the Virginia reel and quadrille (a type of dance for four couples, with each couple forming a single side of a square, it developed from the cotillion, an earlier form of square dance, and became popular in the French court of the early nineteenth century; it was then introduced to London society and became a craze during the mid- to late nineteenth century).

Harriet Lyon Langworthy (daughter of Stephen and Betsey Langworthy) married James Marsh in 1845. Born in New York, he had come west as a surveyor, having surveyed most of Michigan, Wisconsin and Iowa. In 1840, he settled in Dubuque as the U.S. deputy surveyor. He was responsible for surveying the border between Minnesota and Iowa. He used a solar compass when subdividing a large part of the territory around Fort Dodge, Iowa, and also St. Paul and Minneapolis, Minnesota. The solar compass was invented by William Austin Burt in 1835. Rather than depending on magnetic readings, the solar compass used the direction of the sun in terms of its angle relative to the axis of rotation of planet Earth. It, therefore, avoids the problems of magnetic compasses due to erratic readings when in areas of high iron content. The U.S. government chose the solar compass for surveying public lands due to its accuracy. While in Minnesota, Captain Marsh named Lake Harriet for his sweetheart, Harriet Langworthy. The solar compass was on loan from their son, Frank M. Marsh, at the Carnegie Stout Public Library in Dubuque but is no longer located there.

James and Harriet Marsh had one son, Franklin Madison Marsh, who became a civil engineer and roadmaster for the Dubuque & Sioux City Railroad. The Marsh home, built in 1853 at 1049 University Avenue in Dubuque, exuded elegance. Its original Brussels carpet, woven for the home, stretched twenty by forty feet in the Victorian room. The carpet was later donated to the Huntington Library and Art Gallery in San Marino, California. Hand-carved walnut doors with blue Bohemian glass above them welcomed visitors. Inside the home, Corinthian columns supported the concave ceiling of the drawing room. Two large bronze chandeliers arrived from England aboard sailing ships. A mirror that extended the length of the room to a height of thirteen feet had carvings in bamboo covered with gold leaf. The framework for the mirror had come from France. The home possessed eight fireplaces—six of white veined marble and two of pure white Carrara marble from Italy. The outside of the home was constructed of three layers of bricks—from the Langworthy brick works, of course. In later years, the house was owned by Mr. and Mrs. Dale Hayford, the Little Old Lady from Dubuque. Tragically, the magnificent home was demolished in 1965 to make room for an expanding Nativity Church. Today, a modern building housing a radio station occupies the site.

The Langworthy brothers owned six hundred acres in Dubuque. Together, they paid one-twelfth of the entire tax revenue collected in Dubuque during the 1850s. Brigadier General Augustus L. Chetlain of Galena, who was the first to volunteer from Illinois to serve in the Union army during the Civil War and achieved distinction at the Battles of Shiloh and Fort Donelson, wrote *Recollections of 70 Years: Early Galena* in 1893. In this memoir, he stated of the Langworthy brothers, "They are as energetic and wide awake as any to be found." He continued: "Nothing pleased them better than a horse race, turkey shooting match or country dance. They were shrewd, enterprising and industrious." The brothers fostered a very close familial relationship, with parties, anniversaries, birthdays, holidays and hosting each other's families as well as their extended family. One example of their closeness was,

Above: The home of James and Harriet Langworthy Marsh. *From the* Telegraph Herald *(Dubuque, Iowa)*.

Left: Valeria Langworthy's china. *Mathias Ham House Museum, Dubuque, Iowa.*

Valeria Langworthy's china. *Mathias Ham House Museum, Dubuque, Iowa.*

of course, the location of their homes. Another is that each brother bought his wife a set of coordinated engraved Rockingham china from England. Valeria's china, once displayed at the Crystal Palace in London, England, is presently on exhibit at the Ham House Museum in Dubuque.

The story of the Langworthy/Massey families continued through the lives of hundreds of descendants. One example is Ada Langworthy Collier (1843–1919), daughter of Lucius and Valeria Bemis Langworthy. Ada wrote sketches, poems, novels and short stories under the pen names of

"Anna L. Cunningham" and "Marguerite." Even as a child, she created a series of periodicals. She was best known for *Lilith: The Legend of the First Woman* (1885). This long narrative poem examined the legend of Lilith, who had been made by God first as Adam's equal. The clash between Adam and Lilith resulted in Lilith's expulsion from the Garden of Eden and the subsequent creation of Eve. Lilith then married Eblis, who was the prince of devils, and became the mother to demons and specters. In vengeance upon Eve, she developed into the enemy of infants and new mothers, strangling the sleeping babies with a strand of her hair. Collier discovered that the word *lullaby* originates from Lilla or Lilith, so her version of the myth reinvents Lilith. The Lilith of Collier's poem leaves Eden voluntarily rather than submit to dominance, but the cost of this disobedience is the inability to have children. Lilith then steals a baby, who dies in need of its mother—thus the legend of baby killing. Hebrew women traditionally hung four amulets on their nursery walls with the inscription "Lilith be gone" to protect their children from this supposed demon.

Ada Langworthy studied in a school taught by activist Catherine Beecher, daughter of Lyman and Roxanna Beecher and sister of Harriet Beecher Stowe, who wrote *Uncle Tom's Cabin*. Her brothers Henry Ward and Charles Beecher were famous clergymen and ardent abolitionists, along with Catherine and Harriet. Ada graduated from Lasell Seminary in Auburndale, Massachusetts, in 1861 at the age of seventeen. While attending Lasell, she suffered an attack of "brain fever." During the nineteenth century, doctors diagnosed brain fever for several then unknown diseases. She could have had encephalitis, meningitis, cerebritis (inflammation of the cerebrum) or even scarlet fever. Luckily, she survived. She married Robert Hutchinson Collier on October 15, 1867, and had one son, James Currie Collier, born in 1869. Mrs. Collier served as president of the Dubuque Ladies' Literary Association and as an auditor of the Iowa Federation of Women's Clubs. She continued her involvement in Dubuque's civic affairs for the benefit of the community her entire life.

Some of Mrs. Collier's works include *Westward the Star of Empire Takes Its Flight*; *A Series of Hospital Sketches*, written in 1864 and based on material gathered by her on battlefields and hospitals of the Civil War; and *Our Silver Lake Friends*, a children's story. The *Indianapolis Herald* published many of her poetry works. *Chicago Magazine* published "A Country Garden," "A Romance of the Lead Mines," "Dolores" and "My Cousin Dorothy."

James Currie Collier, Ada Langworthy Collier's son, attended Johns Hopkins in Maryland, majoring in chemistry. He intended to follow his father in the family gunpowder business. He managed a mill for the Laflin and Rand Powder Company in New Jersey. His marriage to Susan Adams in 1894 changed his occupational trajectory. In 1895, they returned to Dubuque. Susan Adams Collier's brother and James purchased the Carr, Ryder and Engler Company, which manufactured sash, millwork and doors. Renamed Carr, Adams and Collier Company in 1899, Collier became vice-president. By 1916, he was operating head of the company and president by 1939.

Number 1072 West Third Street is the site of the Collier home, known as Lindencroft. The Queen Anne–style house, designed by Thomas T. Carkeek on land bought from James Langworthy, possessed a grand staircase and beautiful stained-glass windows. The construction of the Collier home included many different woods, as the family had close ties to the city's lumber barons. They used African mahogany, red birch, birdseye maple and quarter-sawn oak to enhance the home's opulence. It is next door to the Robert Collier home, in the same neighborhood as the Edward, Lucius and Solon Langworthy homes.

James Collier's wife, Susan, and her brother, John Taylor Adams (1862–1939), were descendants of presidents John and John Q. Adams. In 1881, Adams began working at Carr, Ryder and Wheeler for three dollars an hour as an office boy. By 1895, he had become president of Carr, Ryder and Adams Company and, later, Carr, Adams and Collier until his death. He served on the board of directors for the First National Bank of Dubuque during the Great Depression of the 1930s. When a run threatened to ruin the bank, he pledged his personal finances to cover the bank's deposits and saved the bank. James Collier, John T. Adams, Charles Spahn, George Rose and James Carr founded the Spahn and Rose Lumber Company in 1904. They were among the first to warn of diminishing lumber supplies in northern Wisconsin, so they purchased lumber holdings on the West Coast, just as Solon Langworthy had done earlier. The Spahn and Rose Lumber Company remains an integral part of Dubuque's business community.

John Taylor Adams worked as the campaign manager for Iowa senator and Dubuque resident William B. Allison. After a trip to Germany prior to World War I amid anti-German hysteria, he was seen as pro-German so was denied the position of chairman of the Republican Party. He continued his active role in the Republican Party and along with his wife often visited the White House and President Calvin Coolidge.

Elizabeth Adams, daughter of John Taylor and Winifred Rose Adams, married George R. Burden in 1924. He was the son of George A. Burden and Viola Ryder. They had established a gentleman's farm on sixty acres of Mississippi River bluffs known as Four Mounds, after their son George contracted polio at the age of fourteen. When Elizabeth died in 1982, she willed the estate to the City of Dubuque. In 1987, the Four Mounds Foundation assumed management of Four Mounds. The acreage, along with its seventeen buildings, was listed in the National Register of Historic Places, and in 2018, a restoration of the grounds to a natural oak savanna was initiated. John Gronen, the grandson of Elizabeth Adams and distant cousin of the Langworthys, returned to Dubuque after a decade's absence in the 1980s. He and his wife started an architectural restoration business in Dubuque. Four Mounds, the Langworthy Octagon House, the Cottingham and Butler Building, the Roshek Building and the Millwork District have been a few of their accomplishments. Many of the ornate, grand and beautiful structures of Dubuque's history have been saved rather than destroyed in the mistaken name of progress by a descendant of some of the city's founders.

Robert Henry Langworthy, great-grandson of Andrew and Rachel Langworthy, was born in 1819. He remained in Rhode Island, unlike his wandering cousins. He studied architecture and in 1843 went into partnership in Westerly, Rhode Island, with his brother William and his cousin Peleg Clarke. It is worth mentioning that the name Peleg occurs in the Langworthy family numerous times. The name is a common surname in Israel and has biblical roots. The original Peleg was the son of Eber in the book of Genesis. The root lettering in Hebrew means sailing—also interesting, as his ancestor was a sailor. Several years later, the business dissolved, and Robert and William formed a new partnership that flourished for thirty-five years. Their firm was regarded as one of the leading architectural firms in Rhode Island, according to Cole's *History of Washington and Kent Counties, Rhode Island*: "[H]is reputation for judgment and honorable and equitable dealings with all associated with him was second to none and he was regarded as one of the leading citizens of Hopkinton and Westerly." Robert married Jennette Potter in 1848 and had one child, Ada, in 1850. Ada married George Noyes Burdick in 1876. They had one son, Henry Langworthy Burdick, in 1879. He graduated from Harvard Law School in 1906.

Charlotte Langworthy (1829–1907), daughter of Stephen and Jane Moureing Langworthy, married Solomon Turck of New York in 1864. Turck had traveled from New York City to St. Louis to improve his fortunes. While there, he worked for Sylvester Laflin in the gunpowder industry. From St. Louis, he moved to Galena and then Platteville, Wisconsin, where he managed the Laflin and Smith Powder Company. The Platteville Mill, located on the Little Platte River, manufactured powder for the Union troops during the Civil War. The company later became the Laflin and Rand Powder Company. Their wagons, commanded by Frank Newton, journeyed overland from Platteville, Wisconsin, to Denver, Colorado, for use in the silver and gold mines of Colorado.

Solomon and his brothers, Titus and John, owned some of the richest silver west of Denver on McClellan Mountain. They also held interests in gold mining. In 1869, Titus Turck married Eugenia Belot of Central City. They later operated a restaurant in Denver. Meanwhile, his brother John sold his interest in the Equator Mine near Georgetown, Colorado, for $100,000 that same year (that would be more than $2 million today).

Robert Collier, who was the husband of Ada Langworthy and son-in-law of Lucius Langworthy, succeeded Solomon Turck as general manager of the Laflin Company. Eventually, the Laflin Powder Mills commanded more than two-thirds of the United States' explosives and gunpowder industry by 1900. Solomon Turck served as mayor of Dubuque in 1868 and 1872. He and Charlotte (or Lottie) moved to New York City when he became president of Laflin-Rand Powder Company, but he always maintained that their happiest days had been in Dubuque. Solomon died of appendicitis/peritonitis, which caused a fatal heart attack on January 30, 1907. A Dubuque fire engine was named in his honor. They had two daughters, Annabel and Florence, and two sons who died in infancy. Annabel married Henry Cohu, but Florence died at age fifteen. Annabel and Henry had two sons, LaMotte Turck and Henry Wallace. Charlotte Langworthy Turck, at the age of eighty-nine, married William Reilly on August 22, 1924, to the shock and amazement of her family. A lawsuit brought against Reilly upon her death eventually resulted in most of her estate being awarded to her family. Charlotte Langworthy Collier Turck died on August 8, 1926.

Both LaMotte and Henry graduated from Princeton University in New Jersey and were listed in the "Elite of New York Society" list of 1915. Henry Wallace Cohu served as an ensign in the U.S. Navy from 1917 to 1919. He then managed Cohu and Company from 1919 to 1956. He became a limited partner in Winslow, Cohu and Stetson Inc. in 1958. He also served as a director of Eastern Industries Inc., Cohu Electronics Inc., Century Investors Inc. and Angostura-Wuppermann Inc. He married Kathryn Kimbal of Madison Avenue, New York City. He died in 1983 and is buried at the Matinecock Friends (Quaker) Meeting House Cemetery in Nassau County, New York. Founded in 1671, the Matinecock Friends Meeting House is the oldest officially organized Friends Meeting House in the United States.

Gissa Bu, the Turck mansion, Southampton, New York. *Wikimedia Commons.*

While attending Princeton, LaMotte Turck Cohu became its lightweight wrestling champion. When the United States entered into World War I, he enlisted in the navy as a fighter pilot. Always having an avid interest in aviation, he worked as an investment broker selling aviation securities after the war.

In 1920, he married Charlotte Adele Guye. She died on February 14, 1923. The next year, on August 30, he married Augustine Didi Muus of Norway. She later became a naturalized citizen of the United States. They had three daughters: Anne, Renee and Marit. Cohu had a summer home built for his wife on Montauk Highway, Southampton, New York, overlooking the ocean with access to the beach. Designed by Norwegian architect Thorbjorn Bassoe and built by Norwegian craftsmen, the home, named Gissa Bu, replicated a medieval Norwegian mountain mansion. According to the Southampton Historic Survey of April 2014, the house had been so intensively renovated that it no longer had historic integrity. However, it sold in 2012 for $3.7 million.

In 1928, LaMotte Cohu formed Air Investors Inc., and in 1930, he organized Interstate Airlines—later a part of Eastern Airlines. He also served as a director of International Telephone and Telegraph Corporation, U.S. Commercial Company and Rubber Development Corporation. He was a founding member of Northrop Aircraft. Begun by John "Jack" Northrop, the aircraft company became an independent company in 1939. It produced dive bombers for England during World War II and the famous Northrop N3PB float plane. The N3PB served out of Iceland after Norway was overrun by Germany in 1940. The float plane patrol and anti-submarine bomber provided protection for North Atlantic convoys. LaMotte Cohu resigned from Northrop when he became president of TWA. Howard Hughes, a close friend of Cohu and the man who controlled TWA, thought that what the airline needed was efficient economic operation of its planes. To get it, he put LaMotte Turck Cohu in as TWA president.

"Tough, canny Mr. Cohu, World War I flyer and ex-board chairman of Northrop Aircraft Inc., lost no time in swinging his new broom—and his ax. He spent so much time flying from one TWA office to another that a TWA underling quipped: 'The loneliest place in the company is the president's office in Kansas City,'" as noted in the April 24, 1947 *Starliner of Trans World Airlines*. But other employees of TWA found nothing humorous in his trips. Wherever Cohu stopped, employees usually got fired:

> *Cohu merged TWA's four regional headquarters into one office and trimmed the airline's swollen staff of 15,000 by 13%. As costs went down and traffic rose, TWA's deficit was turned into a profit of $202,000 in the year's second quarter. The profits rose to $884,000 in the third quarter, promising a gross business of $78,000,000 in 1947 (against $57,000,000 last year). That started Cohu thinking about new planes. The line's once bad credit had improved enough so that fourteen banks put up the $15,000,000 to pay for new planes. TWA had not yet flown through all the rough weather. But the air was smoother than it had been for years.*

In 1948, Cohu moved to Convair Aircraft as president and general manager. The company had formed in 1943 with a merger between Consolidated Aircraft and Vultee Aircraft. It later expanded into rockets and spacecraft, as it had built experimental guided missiles for the armed forces since 1944. Cohu became the general manager of the first factory for the mass production of guided missile weapons that were faster than the speed of sound, located near San Diego, California.

LaMotte Cohu continued working at Cohu Electronics until his death in 1968. He continued flying until 1963. On September 10, 1968, he took his own life in the driveway of his home in San Diego. Tragedy followed the family when his daughter Renee disappeared on January 20, 1970. The wife of investment banker Jack Dana and mother of two sons, she had traveled to San Francisco to attend a friend's funeral. She was to meet her husband there. She never arrived, but her abandoned car was found near Ghirardelli Square on Fisherman's Wharf. Her body was later identified on February 2, 1970, as a Jane Doe who had committed suicide at a Miami, Florida motel.

Her shocked family never knew why she had run away, hid her identity and then ended her own life.

Oella Langworthy, daughter of Stephen and Jane Langworthy Moureing, married Joseph Bennett in 1853. They had two sons before divorcing. She married William Hoffmire in 1877 in Kings, New York. They had one daughter, Elizabeth, in 1881. William Hoffmire worked as a sales agent for the Laflin Rand Powder Company, as did other family members. He died in 1909 while in St. Augustine, Florida. They had traveled there due to his poor health. Oella then lived in Salt Lake City, Utah, where their son lived. She died there in 1922 but is buried at Linwood Cemetery in Dubuque with her parents.

Frederick Isaiah Massey married his cousin Alleen M. Langworthy, daughter of James Langworthy, at the Langworthy home on October 3, 1866. Frederick Massey's father, Dr. Isaiah Frederick Massey, was the brother of Betsey Massey Langworthy. Frederick Massey enlisted in the Union army in 1861 as a first lieutenant in Company I, New York's Ninety-Fourth Regiment. During the war, he was wounded at the Battle of Gettysburg. After the war, he worked for the War Department until 1868. He and Alleen then moved to Dubuque, where he found employment as the auditor for the Chicago, Dubuque & Minnesota Railroad until 1876. Mr. Massey then became the manager of the Dubuque Steam Supply Company.

Dubuque needed a railway connection from the downtown business district to the bluffs of West Dubuque. The problem presented itself as three-hundred-foot-tall bluffs. An engineer hired from New York determined that the grade was too steep for a horse-drawn railcar. The Dubuque Steam Supply Company and Mr. Massey supplied the solution with the *Pioneer*. Burnham, Parry, Williams and Company of Baldwin Locomotive Works in Dubuque built the steam motor, weighing eight and a half tons with steam brakes. The *Pioneer* successfully ascended the hill, drawing cars carrying an average of sixty people. The smokeless, noiseless railway opened on July 25, 1877, with no accidents. Mr. Massey insisted on inspections each hour.

As superintendent of the Hill Street Railway, Mr. Massey invited reporters to be the first to ride on its newest addition, the *Excelsior*, driven by engineer J.S. Lihens. There were no problems. Meanwhile, the company built a new brick engine house with a well, car sheds and a coal shed. Mr. Massey, being "determined to make the railway interesting and attractive," supported Solon Langworthy's construction of a clubhouse. The first story of the clubhouse included ladies' and gentlemen's waiting areas and a refreshment room. The second story featured a dance hall for clubs and private parties, while the third story had a billiard hall for both men and women.

In January 1880, Frederick Massey began work as a contractor for the Holly System of Steam Heating of New York. The Holly Manufacturing Company (1858–1916) had begun by manufacturing sewing machines, pumps and hydraulic equipment. The company diverted excess water from the Erie Canal through an underground tunnel to power a fifty-six-foot-high water turbine wheel to generate 240 horsepower. After a fire struck Lockport, New York, in 1861, while most of its men were off fighting in the Civil War, the Holly Company convinced the city to install fire protection systems in the business district, with hydrants and underground pipes driven by the Holly turbine pump. Birdshill Holly devised a plan to supply the city with water for sanitary and domestic purposes as well as fire protection. By 1881, more than one hundred cities in thirty-five states were using the Holly System of Water Supply and Fire Protection. Denver, Colorado, installed its system in 1880, and it is still functioning today.

In Dubuque, the Holly System established four boilers at its Iowa Street location. Each boiler was sixteen feet long and worked automatically to reduce coal to coke and then feed the fires with the carbonless product. The smokestacks were eighty feet tall. With Frederick Massey as the "driving spirit," the system had ten thousand feet of lines with three thousand more to be laid before winter in 1880. Massey had leased the Mahaska coal mine near Oskaloosa to supply the boilers. The mine employed sixty-five men, who produced 350 tons of coal per day.

After leaving the War Department in 1868 and moving to Dubuque, Mr. Massey also functioned as sales representative for the Massey-Hart Manufacturing Company in Toronto, Canada, owned by his Massey cousins. In 1880, Mr. and Mrs. Massey lived with Mrs. James Langworthy, Alleen's mother, in the family home, Ridgemount. By 1890, he had become the European agent for the Massey-Harris Company living in London, England. They returned to Dubuque every two years. The society pages of the local newspapers were filled with their comings and goings. In 1895, they even traveled to Valparaiso, Chile.

Mr. Massey was a city alderman and served as a first ward delegate to the Dubuque Republican Convention. He bought the Iowa Iron Works in 1882 and served as its vice-president. He and his brother-in-law owned Massey and Langworthy Coal on Iowa Street in Dubuque. He was on the Chicago Board of Trade as well. Both he and his wife supported many philanthropic organizations. Their attendance was necessary at all the balls and celebrations Dubuque had to offer.

Mrs. C.W. Mitchell honored Mrs. Alleen Langworthy Massey at her home on Seventh Street on January 1, 1908, at the meeting of the Dubuque Women's Club. At the meeting, a concise, intelligent and instructive account of the Venezuelan situation was given by eighty-three-year-old Mrs. R. Poor, who was the ex-president of the club. Discussion of current events in science, literature, benevolence, politics and the markets followed. The meeting closed with "dainty refreshments and pleasant conversation." The Dubuque Women's Club started in 1876 as the Dubuque Ladies Literary Association (DLLA). The association defined itself as the "systematic study and mutual improvement" of society. In 1885, Mrs. Massey was the guest of honor at the home of Mrs. R.H. Collier (daughter of Lucius Langworthy) for a meeting of the Ladies Literary Association. One hundred women attended to hear the following speeches after their meal: "The Need of Associations for Women," "An Adamless Eden," "The Pioneer Women of Iowa" and "Old Times and New in Our Association." Obviously, some ideas have not changed since these early days. Mrs. Ada Langworthy Collier and Miss Mary Rogers represented the General Federation of Women's Clubs at the Chicago World's Fair in 1894. Clara Aldrich Cooley of Dubuque represented Iowa at the Paris, France Exposition of 1900 by reading a paper titled "Women in Science." In 1901, the group became the Dubuque Federated Women's Club. The club owns the home at 375 Alpine Street as its headquarters. Some of its achievements involve improved sanitation, parks, a county library and compulsory education laws.

In 1880, Mrs. Massey served on a committee to examine the Grammar Department of the Fourth Ward School (Lincoln Elementary) in Dubuque by assessing the proficiency of the department members as well as the students. They determined that the eleventh class, led by Miss Keneally, demonstrated special proficiency in written arithmetic. They found the entire class working promptly and correctly. The twelfth, thirteenth, fourteenth and fifteenth classes showed high levels of competence in both grammar and American history, while the penmanship of the fourteenth class was worthy of praise. The committee recommended that the school board provide new recitation rooms since the present ones "are small, dark and miserably ventilated." At the Secondary Department of the Fourth Ward School, teachers Miss Cummings, Miss Dixon and Miss Jackson were rated as excellent. Mrs. Massey reported that the students behaved in "good order" and responded to all questions asked with promptness and accuracy. They awarded special notice to Miss Cummings's class for being ahead of their grade level in reading and writing, while Miss Dixon's and Miss Jackson's classes displayed superior knowledge in both geography and mental arithmetic.

Built in 1867, the Fourth Ward School cost $14,556. Unfortunately, the contractor failed to consider the cornices of the roofline, so the walls were four feet too low. In order that the roofline would not cover the upper-story windows, the walls had to be raised at an extra cost of $525. The furniture for the building required an additional expense of $2,012, while the teachers and principal were paid a total of $623. The Fourth Ward School was considered an elaborate and well-appointed school for its time. A name change to the Lincoln School occurred in 1889, when the school board decided to name all the schools after famous Americans. Interestingly, the board allowed Turck (Langworthy son-in-law) and Company to mine under the school for two years beginning in 1892.

All work and no play certainly was not the rule. In February 1878, a Ridotto Hop at the Julien Hotel offered a "magnificent repast" and music by the Union Band despite sleet and snow. (A ridotto is a masquerade dance that was popular in England during the eighteenth century.) Mr. and Mrs. Frederick I. Massey attended the festivity along with other prominent families of the area. Mr. Massey served as secretary of the fraternal benefit society Royal Arcanum, founded in Boston in 1877.

The Masseys traveled the world for the Massey Manufacturing Company. In a scrapbook of souvenirs from Fred Massey, kept by Tom Fiore, there are menus, tickets, business cards and many other items from Brussels, Paris, Algiers, Venice, Prague, Toronto, Lucerne, Perth, Russia, Berlin, Vienna and every other city or country one can name. Mr. Frederick Isaiah Massey died on March 13, 1908, at the Finley Hospital in Dubuque from a brief illness following an appendicitis operation. He is buried at Linwood Cemetery in Dubuque. Mrs. Alleen Langworthy Massey died in Dubuque in 1918.

The J.K. Graves home estate covered four acres on Fenelon Place and apparently was a center of social life. When the Graves family, said to be related by marriage to Dubuque's famed Langworthys, arrived home from New York for a summer visit, the "street buzzed with excitement." People saw and were seen. Parties were lavish and conversation eager. It was a time to be happy and young and excited. Other landed gentry on this personality-filled street knew the format for aristocratic living. But the Graves were the titlists, their old neighbors agreed. Mrs. Graves was said to have "dressed like an empress." The three-story home was demolished to make room for a new home built for Peter Seippel.

Mining was in the blood of many Langworthy family members. According to Harold L. Bischoff in *Clayton's Silica Mine*, John Langworthy was no exception. In 1916, he was said to have started the Langworthy Silica Company in Clayton County, Iowa. Silica was commonly used in plaster for houses, as well as marble cutting and polishing. Foundries also used silica. He had hoped to begin a glass industry in northeast Iowa and even move to Clayton, Iowa, where he planned to build a new home. (No John Langworthy, chiropractor, was found in any source; a mistake may have been made in the original documentation. Solon Massey Langworthy Jr., a chiropractor, was listed along with John Chalmers as president and vice-president of the company when incorporated in 1919.) Silica mining had been occurring in Clayton County since 1878. Prior to that time, the area produced quantities of wheat that were ground into flour at the Motor Mill at Elkader, Iowa. Clayton, founded in 1849, grew rapidly when it became important as a shipping and landing site for the flour. By the 1870s, the region was in a decline due to wheat rust that had arrived from the southern states. The land, exhausted by intensive wheat farming since the 1830s, could no longer support the area farmers. A new economic venture had to be found.

The silica sand deposits from the St. Peter Sandstone formation (464–470 million years old) near Clayton, Iowa, are described as extremely pure. In Iowa, the thickness of the sandstone formation varied from 15 feet to 223 feet. A new industry lay under their feet. Located along the Mississippi River, Clayton had had several silica mining operations. The first was opened in 1878 as an open pit mine by William Buhlman, who found himself in financial trouble when the wheat production business went bankrupt. He hauled the sand in gunnysacks to the train depot, from where they were transported to glass factories in Milwaukee. His workers were earning fifty cents an hour by the time it closed in 1929. The second business, operated by Richard Kolck of Dubuque, manufactured bricks from 1919 to 1929; the third and most extensive was the Langworthy operation. When workers began removing sand from the bluffs, they found five rooms carved out of the sandstone, with passageways connecting them. Four of the rooms were destroyed despite attempts by local citizens to save them. It remains unknown who carved these rooms or when.

Judge Chalmers, Solon Massey Langworthy Jr., Ed Beaman and Otto Lange, all of Dubuque, formed the board of directors for the Langworthy

Langworthy Mine, Clayton, Iowa. *Bob Libra, state geologist, Iowa Department of Natural Resources.*

Silica Company, with Harvey Lange (Otto's son) as manager. They employed eight to twenty men, with ten railroad cars of wet sand shipped out of Clayton per day. The mine's activity had to be reduced in the winter when the sand froze. In the 1930s, the John Deere Company urged them to sell dry sand. With John Deere's business to support the investment, the mine added a dryer and began selling dry sand. Since wet sand sold for $0.80 per ton but dry sand sold for $1.75 per ton, they determined the dryer to be a good investment.

During World War II, the U.S. government imposed price and wage controls to prevent price gouging and to ensure a supply of necessary materials for the war effort. As a result, the Langworthy Mining Company could not offer the same pay increases as newly opened mines, which were not under the same price constraints. Langworthy's workers quit for higher-paying jobs, and the mine shut down. After the war ended in 1945, Concrete Materials Company leased the pit and started the process of room and pillar underground mining. The Martin Marietta Corporation bought the Concrete Materials Company in 1959 and continued to lease the Langworthy Mine. The underground operation expanded to fourteen miles of tunnels with sixty acres of storage. The tunnels cut 2,300 feet into the bluffs and 3,200 feet along the river at 250 feet from the surface. During the Cold War, the mine became a site for a nuclear war shelter. It held the capacity for forty-four thousand people with ten railroad cars and ten semi-trailers loaded with medical supplies, food and water. The major obstacle to this plan concerned the fact that only one road ran to the mine. One plan was to have a car drive to the mine and then the next car would push the first car into the river and so on—not very practical, but these were not practical times.

In 1982, Pattison Brothers purchased the mine from the Langworthy and Chalmers families. They began storing fertilizer and other commodities in the mine. Today, silica sand is used in the hydraulic fracturing process of extracting oil and natural gas. In 2016, Pattison Sand Company expanded the mine to 746 acres.

Pauline Langworthy (daughter of Edward and Paulina) married George Welles Rood in 1879. They had one daughter, Eleanor Langworthy Rood, born in 1880. She married John George Chambers in 1904. They had six children, four of whom survived to adulthood. They established their home in the Langworthy Octagon House built by her grandfather on West Third Street. The home featured thirteen rooms, with space for one hundred guests to attend a tea party and eighty for a formal dinner.

Born in Downsville, New York, on August 17, 1874, George Chalmers arrived in Dubuque in 1901. A recent graduate of Lafayette College in Easton, Pennsylvania, he took a teaching position in history and math at Dubuque Senior High School while also coaching football. That year, his team won the Iowa State Championship. The next year, he returned to Pennsylvania to coach and assume the duties of athletic director for Lancaster schools. Iowa lured him back with a position at the University of Iowa in Iowa City. There he worked as director of physical education and athletics, as well as coached football, baseball, basketball and track. As if that were not a busy enough schedule, he enrolled in the University of Iowa Law School. By 1906, he had married Eleanor Langworthy Rood and had begun practicing law in Dubuque.

Coaching, he decided, must remain a hobby. Columbia College (Loras) hired him as its football coach in 1907. He stayed there six years—so much for the hobby idea. The University of Dubuque coaxed him to join it in 1914. He coached football and then became its first baseball coach. He stayed at the University of Dubuque until 1925—all the while he also practiced law. In 1919, Mr. Chalmers served as the referee in bankruptcy for the Northern District of Iowa, Eastern Division. A referee in bankruptcy was a federal official with quasi-judicial powers who was appointed by a U.S. court to administer bankruptcy proceedings prior to 1979. In March 1942,

Eleanor Langworthy Rood, granddaughter of Edward and Paulina Langworthy. *Brad Chalmers.*

Mr. Chalmers became Judge Chalmers with his appointment as judge of the Nineteenth District by Governor George A. Wilson. Chalmers became the first Republican to ever hold that position since the office had been created in 1887; he maintained his appointment until retirement in 1955.

The University of Dubuque honored Judge Chalmers by naming the athletic field Chalmers Field in 1945. President Dale Welch said of Chalmers and his commitment to the university, "We set aside these thirty acres of land as Chalmers Field in memory of the great work of a great man, and in anticipation of the years of service that this area and its equipment will be put to in the future." A former student described Chalmers: "He was brilliant in all his abilities but never seeking praise—an inspiration to his associates."

Eleanor Langworthy Rood Chalmers died on August 18, 1917, shortly after the birth of their youngest son, Bruce. Tragically, Bruce died at the age of nineteen as a result of an auto accident on the way to the family cottage in northern Wisconsin.

John Chalmers married Rose Nussbaum of Indiana in 1921. She said of herself, "Music has been my life." She was the head of the University of Dubuque Voice Department and director of the Westminster Presbyterian Church Choir. At the age of ten, she had joined with her sister and brothers in a quartet called the Nightingales. They performed at the Chicago World's Fair in 1893 at the request of the Indiana governor. She studied music in Chicago and then toured the Chautauqua circuit in the early 1900s. After moving to California, she joined a quartet known as the Pacific Ladies. After she came to the University of Dubuque, she often sang at patriotic rallies during World War I and performed at the Grand Opera House. Her last performance occurred when she sang *The Mikado* at the University of Dubuque the night before her wedding to John Chalmers. After the wedding, Mr. and Mrs. Chalmers lived in the family home on West Third Street with the four Chalmers children. Eventually, Edward Langworthy Chalmers and his family lived in the main house, and Judge and Mrs. Chalmers lived in the new wing that had been added to the back of the house.

Judge Chalmers, an avid conservationist, along with Paul Smith and Walter Bade, advised the U.S. War Department on the development and use of eight thousand acres between Guttenberg and Bellevue, Iowa, as a recreation/conservation area. Chalmers also belonged to the Dubuque Conservation Society, the Rotary Club and the Dubuque Chamber of Commerce. As president of the Conservation Society, Judge Chalmers attended an Arbor Day program at Marshall School on April 16, 1946, on Rhomberg Avenue in Dubuque. As part of the program, the Conservation Society donated a tree for the school grounds. Judge Chalmers served as president of the Iowa State Cancer Society, for which he sponsored numerous fundraising drives, and was on the board of directors of the Dubuque Abstract Company and the Langworthy Silica Company. In 1962, the Dubuque Real Estate Board awarded him the Outstanding Citizen honor. As a final tribute to his contributions to both the city and the university, the university named Judge Chalmers to the University of Dubuque Hall of Fame in 1991.

Judge Chalmers died on June 8, 1962. Rose Nussbaum Chalmers died on September 4, 1962. Both are buried at Linwood Cemetery, Dubuque, Iowa. The Edward Langworthy Octagon House remains in private family ownership.

CONCLUSION

*T*he Langworthy family arrived in the Rhode Island Colony in 1652. Their journey to newer lands eventually brought them to Dubuque. Their story is the story of the early United States, from colonization to revolution to westward movement to mining rushes and beyond. They endured the physical hardships, tragedies and failures of all frontier settlers. They became business owners, farmers, bankers and manufacturers, as had so many others who ventured forth for a better life in the Midwest.

The risks that they took helped to establish not only their own families but also towns, cities and states. They were present at the founding of the United States, the rescue of the nation during the Civil War and every other major national event in its history. Many of their descendants continued to display the traits of hard work, entrepreneurship, family loyalty, philanthropy and risk-taking.

The Langworthy family deserves to be called "Dubuque's First Family" for all its contributions to the city. It is difficult to imagine the Dubuque of today, the state of Iowa, the Midwest or, in fact, the United States without the Langworthys of yesterday.

BIBLIOGRAPHY

Books

Allison, Nathaniel Thompson. *History of Cherokee County, Kansas and Representative Citizens*. Chicago, 1904.

Becket, Hugh W. *The Montreal Snow Shoe Club: Its History and Record*. Montréal, CN: Becket Brothers, 1882.

Becknell, Thomas Williams. *History of the State of Rhode Island and Providence Plantations*. New York: American Historical Society, 1920.

Bradsby, Henry C., ed. *History of Bureau County, Illinois*. Chicago: World Publishing Company, 1885.

Brigham, Johnson. *Iowa History and Its Foremost Citizens*. Vol. 1. Chicago: S.J. Clarke Publishing Company, 1918.

Chetlain, Augustus L. *Recollections of 70 Years: Early Galena*. N.p.: Gazette Publishing Company, 1899.

Cole, J.R. *History of Washington and Kent Counties, Rhode Island*. New York: Preston & Company, 1889.

Day, Edward Warren. *One Thousand Years of Hubbard History, 1866–1895*. New York: Harland Page Hubbard, 1895.

Hellert, Susan Miller. *Hidden History of Dubuque*. Charleston, SC: The History Press, 2016.

History of Dubuque County. Chicago: World Publishing Company, 1880.

Iowa History from Earliest Times to the Beginning of the 20ᵗʰ Century. Vol. 3. New York: Century History Company, n.d.

Kruse, Len. *My Old Dubuque: Collected Writings on Dubuque Area History.* Dubuque, IA: Center for Dubuque History, Loras College, 2000.

Langworthy, William Franklin. *The Langworthy Family; Some Descendants of Andrew and Rachel (Hubbard) Langworthy Who Were Married at Newport Rhode Island, November 3, 1658.* Hamilton, NY: William F. and Otello S. Langworthy, 1940.

Mahoney, Timothy. *From Hometown to Battlefield in the Civil War Era: Middle Class Life in Midwest America.* Lincoln: University of Nebraska, 2016.

North American Family Histories, 1500–2000. Vol. 84. Daughters of the American Revolution Lineage Book.

Richman, Irving Berdine. *Ioway to Iowa: Genesis of a Corn and Bible Commonwealth.* State Historical Society of Iowa, 1931.

Ullrich, Laura Thatcher. *The Age of Homespun: Objects and Stories in the Creation of an American Myth.* New York: Vintage Books, 2001.

Newspapers

Bismarck (ND) Daily Tribune.
Cascade Pioneer.
Cedar Rapids Evening Gazette.
Council Bluffs Nonpareil.
Des Moines Register.
Dubuque Daily Express and Herald.
Dubuque Daily Herald.
Dubuque Daily Telegraph.
Dubuque Enterprise.
Dubuque Herald.
Dubuque Sunday Herald.
Dubuque Telegraph Herald.
Dubuque Weekly Express Herald.
Dubuque Weekly Times.
The Gazette (Cedar Rapids).
Iowa City Press Citizen.
Mason City Globe Gazette.
Monticello (IA) Express.
Pomona Progress Bulletin Southland.
Potosi Republican. 1848.
Press-Telegram (Long Beach, California).

Santa Anna Register (*Orange County Register*).
Sunday Gazette and Republican (Cedar Rapids, Iowa).
Telegraph Herald and Times Journal.
Weekly Register-Call (Black Hawk, Colorado).
Wisconsin Herald.

Journals and Articles

Allen, June. "Stories in the News." *Sit News*, November 24, 2002.
Bischoff, Harold L. "Clayton's Silica Mine." *The Palimpsest* 55, no. 3 (n.d.): 84–97.
Chiropractic History 1, no. 1. "Solon Massey Langworthy Jr." (1981).
Gebhard, David, and Gerald Monsheim. "Edward Langworthy House." *Society of Architectural Historians Archipedia* (n.d.).
The Iowa Journal of History and Politics 8, no. 3 (July 1910). Published quarterly by the State Historical Society of Iowa, Iowa City, Iowa.
Jacobsen, James. "Phase V Dubuque Historical and Architectural Survey of Fenelon Place, North Mine and Broadway Streets." *Journal of History and Politics* 8 (June 30, 2005).
Owens, David Dale. "Report of a Geological Exploration of Part of Iowa, Wisconsin, Illinois." *House Executive Document no. 239*. Washington, D.C.: Glaire and Rives Printer, 1845.
Southampton Historic Survey (April 2014).
Starliner of Trans World Airlines. April 24, 1947.
Thompson, William H. "Transportation in Iowa: A Historical Summary." 1989. Iowa Department of Transportation.
Time. "Aeronautics: Cohu for Coburn." March 28, 1932.

Websites

Ancestry.com.
The Biographical Dictionary of Iowa. University of Iowa Press, Digital Division. http://uipress.lib.uiowa.edu/bdi.
British Library Collection. bl.uk/collection-items.
Chicago, Illinois and Iowa Biographical Dictionary. Via ancestry.com.
Encyclopedia Dubuque. www.encyclopediadubuque.org.
Mayo Clinic. www.mayoclinic.org.

Perry, Michael. *A Territorial Period Site in Dubuque*. The Office of the State Archaeologist, University of Iowa Digital Division. http://uipress.lib.uiowa.edu/bdi.

Rootsweb. http://www.rootsweb.com.

Miscellaneous Sources

Center for Dubuque History, Loras College. Dubuque, Iowa.

Chalmers, Brad. Interview with author, multiple texts and phone calls, various dates.

Diane Gibson Family Archives.

Dolan, Brennen. Iowa DOT Office. Ames, Iowa.

Edward Langworthy Memoir. Loras College, Center for Dubuque History.

Fiore, Tom. Travels of Frederick I. Massey scrapbook. Loras College, Center for Dubuque History.

George Parrot affidavit, notarized by Eugene Kean. September 11, 1939. Personal collection of Diane Gibson.

Ham House Museum, Dubuque, Iowa.

Iowa Geological Survey.

Langworthy, Lucius. *Sketches of Early Settlement of the West*. Speech, Iowa.

Lucius Langworthy, Speeches and Lectures. 1854 and 1855. Loras College, Center for Dubuque History.

National Mississippi River Museum and Aquarium Archives.

National Park Service. *The Stampede North: The Alaska Gold Rushes, 1897–1904*. Brochure.

Northrup Annual Report, 1946–47. Available via salsburyscooterscrapbooks.com.

Putnam Museum and Science Center, Davenport, Iowa.

Solon Langworthy Diary. National Mississippi River Museum and Aquarium Archives.

Wainwright, Mecalla. Interview with author, July 15, 2021.

Wisconsin Historical Society.

ABOUT THE AUTHOR

Susan Miller Hellert has also published *Hidden History of Dubuque*. Susan lives on the Miller Family Heritage Farm (owned by the same family for more than 150 years) in Dubuque County. She is a retired senior lecturer in the History Department at the University of Wisconsin–Platteville. Always fascinated by local history, she wrote a local history column for the *Dubuque Telegraph Herald* and gives talks and school programs to enhance residents' knowledge of local history. The family farm includes a restored 1880s log cabin built by Susan's great-grandfather and a barn built of lumber from the dismantled roller coaster in Union Park of Dubuque County. She and her family raise a variety of animals for food and fiber. Spinning wool, weaving, knitting, gardening, horseback riding and reading occupy her "free" time.

Visit us at
www.historypress.com